A Group Called
Women

A Group Called
Women

Sisterhood & Symbolism in the Feminist Movement

Joan Cassell

David McKay Company, Inc.   New York

A Group Called Women:
Sisterhood and Symbolism in the Feminist Movement

Developmental Editor: Nicole Benevento
Design: Leslie Bauman
Manufacturing and Production Supervisor: Donald W. Strauss
Composition: Adroit Graphic Composition Inc.
Printing and Binding: Haddon Craftsmen

Library of Congress Cataloging in Publication Data

Cassell, Joan.
A group called women.

Includes bibliographical references and index.
1. Feminism—United States.   2. Feminism—New York
(City).   I. Title.
HQ1426.C28   301.41′2′0973   76-58837
ISBN 0-679-30331-6

To Eric, Who Made Everything Possible

. . . we know already the chief problem and that is that most women still don't identify themselves as a group called women.

—Jill Johnston, 1973

Up to now, the sociological position of the individual woman had certain peculiar elements. The most general of her qualities, the fact that she was a woman and as such served the functions proper to her sex, caused her to be classified with all other women under one general concept. It was exactly this circumstance which removed her from the processes of group-formation in their strict sense, as well as from actual solidarity with other women. . . .

In recent years, women have placed themselves in direct opposition to men in aiming at equalization in all these respects, and occasionally they have succeeded in such matters as personal position and economic independence, intellectual attainment and consciousness of self, in their freedom in society, and in their role in public life. A differentiation from men along party-lines, which emphasized the solidarity of interests among women, becomes noticeable as soon as their basic dissimilarity as over against men decreases with regard to their ways of life, their interest-orientation, and in terms of the law. These party alignments (of women against men) are both cause and consequence of this development. . . .

This is, then, an extraordinary clear-cut case of group-formation on a higher level, which is based on the fact that members are brought together by a general concept. Previously, each of the members had been confined to a single group; now the new group emancipates them from this confining relationship.

—Georg Simmel, 1922

Preface

Unlike traditional anthropological studies, where the observer is presented as one of the few authorities on what happens among a distant and exotic group, this book discusses a contemporary urban social movement with which readers have some familiarity. It is therefore easier for them to challenge my observations and interpretations. I cannot even present myself as an "objective" observer. Unlike traditional anthropological fieldwork, where there is a cultural and emotional gulf between the group observed and the visiting observer, I was part of the research population and was involved in the phenomenon I examined. As an urban white middle-class woman, born and raised in New York City, I was observing other urban, primarily white, middle-class women in the New York City area. In addition, I was not studying "subjects" or even statistics. My observation was highly participative; I learned by doing—joining groups, "rapping" with other women, arguing theory, and taking part in demonstrations and confrontations. Consequently I believe it is particularly important for me to spell out exactly where I stand vis-à-vis the women's movement, so that readers can discount for my biases.

First, let me state that I do not think I would have become involved in the women's movement if it had not been the topic of my Ph.D. dissertation. I have been interested in other movements and organizations; I have read their literature and sent them contributions. But I am not a joiner. I am an observer by nature. That may be one reason I became an anthropologist.

I was receptive to feminism, however, because I wanted to know why my interests as a person and the needs of my children seemed to conflict, and I hoped the women's movement had some answers. In 1960 I had used my first pregnancy as an excuse to leave my job as an advertising copywriter. This was entirely my decision. I continued to free-lance for the advertising agency where I had been employed, however, earning nearly as much as my husband did as a full-time Fellow at a medical school.

In those days, there seemed to be a three-way division of people at parties: the men would talk "man-talk" in one corner, with a few seductive or "man-talk-type" women joining them; one group of women would sit in another part of the room discussing babies and recipes; and in a third group were more women, who discussed their jobs and babies. Moving between the two female groups—I qualified for each and was interested in the subject matter of each—I noticed something interesting. Unasked, each housewife voluteered copious reasons why she had decided not to work, bolstering these with cautionary tales of neglected children of working mothers. The working mothers, in turn, took care to describe how "well adjusted" their children were, and expressed satisfaction that they weren't bores like some women they knew. Why was each group so defensive? It added up to a double-bind situation. A woman could not win—especially since both groups agreed that childless women were missing the meaning of life.

After the birth of my second child and a flirtation with French cooking—I gained thirteen pounds and a reputation as a good cook—I realized that my interests had contracted to a space not much larger than my home and family. I was beginning to bore not only my husband—he told me so—but even myself. I then went back to school. Looking at my application to graduate school, I note it says I was interested in "women's self-images."

During a summer of fieldwork training in the West Indies, I thought of studying the way Jamaican women seemed to be able to leave children and husband, to take a job or get further schooling, without appearing to suffer from the kind of guilt that paralyzed so many middle-class American women. There were not enough such women in the Jamaican town where I was working, so the project was shelved.

The interest in women's lives and self-images, and in the apparent conflict between individual growth and the needs of children, remained, however, and when my graduate adviser, after recommending several "serious" anthropological dissertation topics (suitable for a married woman with two children who could not leave New York City), jokingly suggested I study "Women's Lib," I was awake most of the following night, returning to ask him if I really could study "Women's Lib." "Sure," he replied. "Why not?" So I did.

In studying the women's movement, I went through the process described in part 1: I became a feminist and began to identify myself as a member of a group composed of women. The following is a quote from my field notes, after four months of participation in the women's movement:

> I guess my consciousness is being raised. At the meeting [of a scientific group I attended as my husband's wife], the President made a "slip" while introducing a new research associate, saying she was "all things to all people." He then tried to remedy this, getting in deeper, saying "she does just what anyone asks her to do." There was general laughter among the primarily male audience, with a few remarks about "Gee, I know what I'd like to ask her to do!" For the first time in my life I publicly reacted

and said in a piercing voice: "This laughter insults women!" The laughter stopped almost immediately.

My feelings about women changed: I began to value female friendship more and to take more pleasure in the company of women. My feelings about men, however, did not change. The women's movement added a dimension to my life; it took nothing from me. My marriage did not change. In a consciousness-raising group I joined (one of four such groups), the women spent much time discussing the domestic division of labor, with reports of household lists, arguments, and active and passive resistance by husbands and lovers. Although several members tried to convince me that I should demand that my husband share equally in household and child-care tasks, I refused. My husband worked days and nights; I felt his work as a physician was more important than mine; and an ultimatum such as share-the-work-or-else must have a powerful threat behind it. I was not willing to risk my marriage for a principle that was less important to me than the marriage itself. One member was especially condemnatory; she told me that hiring household help to do one's "shitwork" was "politically incorrect," and when I explained that I could not do my work with a house and two children to care for, and no help, she retorted, "Well, you're the one who got yourself into this; now you'll just have to deal with the consequences!" This (childless) feminist seemed to interpret my attitude as a direct personal threat; she felt I should be angry at my husband, or at least resentful.

This, then, was a limit to my feminism. I chose my marriage, including a conventional division of labor, rather than trying to rearrange my household and my life according to feminist principles. Those who measure feminism by the degree of separation from men, or by the "politics of housework," may find me a half-baked feminist.

Acknowledgments

The topic of this study was first suggested by Lambros Comitas, and although I suspect he regarded my research with mild amusement and some dismay, he was always helpful and his comments were invariably perceptive, intelligent, and supremely practical. Margaret Mead has been an inspiration as long as I can remember: I was introduced to her work in high school; was fortunate to study fieldwork techniques with her as a graduate student; and benefited from her incomparable expertise and experience during the fieldwork period.

I am grateful to the National Institute of Mental Health for a predoctoral fellowship and to the Business and Professional Women's Foundation for the Lena Lake Forrest Fellowship, which provided funds for field research and writing my dissertation.

My research was greatly facilitated by the women's liberation ideology of sisterhood, which includes a belief that women should help and support one another. The feminists among whom I worked were generous with such support. To give only two examples: When Sarah Miller, who was interviewed in detail about her career in the women's movement, was checking the material about herself, she requested just one change—that I put back a quotation I had deleted about her husband having had an extramarital affair. "I think it might help other women to know this," she said. And Mary Gallagher, with whom I had talked by telephone but never met, xeroxed her entire dissertation and mailed it to me when I was unable to obtain a copy; with the dissertation came a note urging me not to repay her for copying it, if it were at all difficult for me to do so. This attitude of warmth and support for other women was widespread in the movement. I hope I can pass it on personally and professionally.

I am grateful to Rosalie Wax, Murray Wax, Elinor Barber, Victor Turner, and Michelle Rosaldo for criticism, suggestions, and encouragement. Murray Wax helped me prepare the manuscript for publication, juggling scattered pieces of paper, disjointed footnotes, and scrambled clauses with competence and good humor.

It is difficult to describe adequately the emotional and intellectual sustenance provided by my husband, Eric, throughout the years spent as graduate student, fieldworker, and writer. He has always expected more from me than I thought myself capable of, and his love, strength, encouragement and steadfast belief have enabled me to learn and grow—as an anthropologist and as a person.

Contents

Introduction

This is a study of group formation and organization among women, based on field research conducted between September 1971 and June 1973 in the New York City area. It explores the process of becoming a feminist, of defining oneself as a member of a group composed of women; and it examines the structure of the women's movement. In this book I view the women's movement as an informally organized interest group whose structure is articulated through symbolic patterns and activities.[1] Central to this feminist symbolism is an opposition between the communal attributes of sisterhood and the coercive and hierarchical behaviors attributed to men.

Part 1 describes the process of becoming a feminist. The focus is on women joining a new interest group, with subsequent changes in self-definition, group affiliation, beliefs, and behaviors. A feminist perceives women as a group or class. The perception of such a group, and of oneself as a member of it, is necessary for a woman to define herself as a feminist and to be so defined by others. This section begins with an analysis of the phrase "raised consciousness," proceeding to receptivity and involvement, consciousness-raising groups, changing relationships with women and men, becoming a lesbian, and feminist demeanor and sexual deference.

There are many determinants to a woman becoming a feminist; some operate in certain situations and not in others. Similarly, there are many ways of becoming a feminist; there is no standard route. Consequently, the description here is generalized: I am examining a journey, or "moral career." [2] Despite the fact that the term "raised consciousness" refers to a subjective state, one sees tangible changes when a woman becomes a feminist. Although alterations in self-image and interpersonal relationships may not be apparent to outsiders, other more visible changes parallel these altered relationships with self and with others. The new feminist dresses differently, walks differently, talks differently. She behaves differently toward women and toward men. She no longer accords men the kind of sexual deference that is so taken for granted in our society in male-female relations that it is noticeable primarily when absent. This behavior (which is more common among the women's liberation branch of the women's movement) may not be overtly identified by outsiders, who nevertheless react strongly to it; the revolutionary feminist is perceived as rude, overbearing, "castrating," and masculine. Women's liberation demeanor tends to elicit hostile and repressive measures, thus acting as a self-fulfilling prophecy, reinforcing a woman's rejection of the nonfeminist world.

Part 1 of this book, then, outlines the steps toward sisterhood, concentrating on an individual joining a new interest group. Feminism, however, consists of more than a category or conceptual group; the women's movement is composed of a large number of groupings and organizations seeking to elevate the status of women. Part 2 examines these groups. In chapter 7, the division of the movement into two branches, which I call women's rights and women's liberation, is discussed and the differences between the two branches are examined. Pragmatic women's rights organizations have traditional bureaucratic structures, with elected officers, boards of directors, bylaws, membership rules, and so forth. This is a familiar form which presents few conceptual difficulties. Utopian women's liberation groupings, on the other hand, are organized by symbolic strategies rather than by formal structure; in fact, one of these strategies is a rejection of "structure." This is a less familiar form than a traditional bureaucratic organization, raising interesting theoretical questions.

Women's liberation and women's rights groups differ in structure, means, goals, and operating procedures. Nevertheless, they define themselves as part of the same social movement. The view of a social movement as an informally organized interest group composed of a variety of units with disparate structures, goals, procedures, and principles of operation is possible only with a processual multigroup model of social movements. The structure of the women's movement is examined in chapter 8, using such a multigroup model. The observed structure of the movement is then discussed in light of various theories and classifications of social movements. It becomes apparent that social movements can be composed of units that differ in almost every conceivable way. What is problematic is not diversity but unity: we must explore the way segments are joined despite differences.

The women's movement is unified by a dominant symbolic form based on a belief in "the women's way" as opposed to "the way men do things." Chapter 9 presents a case study of a women's liberation group, with an examination of its operating principles. These include a rejection of structure, leadership, individual authority, and individual decision making. Women's liberationists contrast these principles with the structured, authoritarian, hierarchical way men operate (sometimes called "masculine structure"). Similar concepts can be found in more formally organized women's rights groups, where feminism is frequently defined in terms of a less structured, coercive, hierarchical pattern than "the way men do things." Thus, a basic component of this dominant feminist symbolism is a rejection of power and hierarchy. A central function of an interest group, however, is to protect or increase the collectivity's share of power.[3] We find, then, the basic contradiction of an interest group whose function is to maximize power organizing itself in terms of a rejection of power. The symbolism that defines the group's distinctiveness, when taken as a rule for behavior, limits its instrumental effectiveness. As a consequence, utopian women's liberation groupings, which originated the symbolic strategy that defines the entire collectivity, and which attempt to follow its rules, achieve fewer measurable results; pragmatic women's rights organizations, who believe in the symbolism but violate the rules, are more likely to achieve tangible political gains. One type of group provides the symbolism that organizes the entire movement; the other works to increase power and benefits for the collectivity.

A process of change comparable to the widening ripples that appear when a pebble is tossed into the water is investigated in chapter 11. This ripple effect is evident in the lives of feminists, in feminist organizations, in the spread of the movement geographically and through social classes: as the outer ripples spread, the center dissolves. Although the book is written in the "ethnographic present," referring to the fieldwork period (1971 through 1973), this section follows the ripple effect through more recent manifestations.

At this point I should state that I had some difficulties with the ethnographic present, which conveys a false effect of timelessness particularly inappropriate for a social movement whose most consistent feature is rapid change, but I have used this technique because I believe that feminism follows certain invariant phases.[4] Although timing differs, so that women who have become feminists, and feminist groupings, in, say, New York City, are in a later stage, while in, say, Miami, individuals and groups have just come to the earliest stage, I think the sequence itself is fixed: one stage follows another wherever the movement occurs. Therefore, despite the fact that the ethnographic present no longer describes the current situation in New York City, I believe it applies to feminism and feminists in areas where the women's movement is more recent.

The uneasy relationship between feminism and the nuclear family is examined in chapter 12. As the title indicates, this chapter consists more of questions than answers.

Throughout the book, all quotations and observations that are not attributed to a particular author come from my field notes. Although I attempted to record what people said as accurately as possible, these quotations are approximate (since they were generally recorded after the occasion).

Because this work is based primarily on my field research, I have not included a history of the contemporary women's movement. Excellent accounts of the formation of both branches of the movement can be found in books by Ware, Freeman, and Hole and Levine.[5]

FIELD METHODS

This study is based on participant observation of a range of women's movement activities and organizations; interviews with feminists; a written questionnaire distributed to participants in a women's liberation group; interaction measurements taken during meetings of the women's liberation group; and analysis of feminist articles, newsletters, pamphlets, and books.

Participant observation provided the basic understanding of the dynamics, values, and structure of the women's movement. Starting in September 1971, I spent two months as a volunteer at the Women's Liberation Center in Manhattan, answering phones and letters, distributing movement literature, and giving information on feminist services available in New York. The Women's Center was then staffed by two part-time workers augmented by volunteer help. Informants said that lesbians were "running" the Center at this time, and observation supported this claim. Volunteers and visitors who were "gay" (not all were) made no attempt to conceal their sexual orientation or activities, and there was much discussion among regular volunteers of lesbian events, bars, and relationships. I was not made to feel uncomfortable because I was "straight"—although one woman said with interest when I admitted, in response to her question, that I was married: "Oh, wow! You're the only married person I practically know!" The Women's Center provided an introduction to women's liberation ideas, organizations, and individuals. On the front door was a poster with a circle extolling sisterhood, and a prohibition against men entering; these themes were encountered frequently during my subsequent fieldwork.

During this introductory period, I also volunteered to help at the New York office of the National Organization for Women (NOW). Unlike the Women's Liberation Center, which was in a loft in a warehouse section of Manhattan, the NOW office was then located in a fashionable upper East Side neighborhood. The president of the chapter said she believed women would not come to "out of the way" places. NOW had no paid office staff or daily volunteers; consequently, when the president was not there answering phones and letters, there was no one to let volunteers in to work. Despite the fact that there was a poster prominently displayed in the NOW office exhorting women not to be exploited by doing volunteer work, NOW wanted volunteers, and one morning, while I was unsuccessfully attempting to get into the NOW office to work, my husband received a phone call asking me to list the days and hours per month I was willing to devote to NOW office work. After several occasions when I showed up and could not get into the office, I stopped going to NOW.

In October 1971 I attended my first weekly meeting of the university action group. I was to attend regularly during the next two school years. Almost by accident, I became involved with a subcommittee that turned out to be at the hub of that year's action-group activities, with a cause célèbre that rallied other campus groups and generated a series of emergency meetings, rallies, demonstrations, press conferences, leaflets, and so forth. It was exciting but time-consuming: a participant could spend every evening and weekend on special meetings and work details and, indeed, many activists did just that. In fact, it was essential to devote much time to group projects if one wanted to be part of the central core of activists.

I attended two meetings of a NOW committee on the media and a public NOW consciousness-raising session. I discovered, however, that it was impossible to be an active member of the university group, belong to a consciousness-raising group, and be active in NOW during the same time period. Meetings were generally held in the evening, and there are only so many evenings per week. When a decision between women's rights and women's liberation appeared necessary, I chose to concentrate on the women's liberation branch for emotional and theoretical reasons—which were, in fact, related. Although I more closely resembled the women's rights members I met—in demographic measures such as age, marital status, husband's profession, socioeconomic status—the women's liberation ideology of sisterhood was powerful and compelling—an ideology the participants seemed to try to live up to. The activists in the university group were close to one another: they helped each other and worked to help other women. In addition, a group that appeared to have (as its members said of it) no leadership or structure had great theoretical interest. Consequently, I became an active participant-observer in the women's liberation branch of the movement.

It was during participant observation in the university action group that I found an interesting divergence between what the women said, and appeared to believe, they were doing and observed behavior. Perceptions of this difference were sharpened during interviews with fifteen women's suffragists, aged seventy-seven to ninety-one, who described to me what they thought they had been doing more than fifty years ago when they worked for the vote for women. (The data from these interviews were not comparable with the direct observations of today's women's movement and were consequently omitted from this study. Exposure to an earlier generation of feminists, however, added perspective to my examination of contemporary group formation among women.)

I also carried out participant observation among four consciousness-raising groups. Each met one evening a week. The first group, which was affiliated with the university action group, dissolved after two and a half months. The second group was still meeting when I left after six months; this group had no ties with other movement organizations. I attended meetings of the third group for two months. This group was composed of the remainder of a consciousness-raising group that had split, after which three women placed a notice in the Women's Liberation Center, seeking new members. Although this group had no formal ties to other movement organizations, members were more militant than the women in the second group.

After announcing, at the first meeting I attended of each of these three groups, that I was a graduate student working on a dissertation on feminism, I took part in group activities in the same way as the other members: I outlined my life history, discussed my feelings about women and men, answered personal questions as honestly as I could, and battled over ideology and feelings. Of course, unlike every other member, I carefully wrote down as complete a description as possible of what went on, the following morning.

I was somewhat more of an observer than a participant in the fourth consciousness-raising group, whose meetings I attended for two months. This group had a leader, and her permission enabled me to attend meetings; it was not necessary to join the group and be a participating member. This group, which was devoted to "leadership training" and was more therapeutic in tone than the other three, had informal ties with NOW: the leader and members helped run monthly NOW public consciousness-raising sessions; women who phoned NOW about consciousness raising during the spring of 1972 were referred to the leader; and the majority of group members also belonged to NOW. This group was eventually dissolved by the leader, who announced that henceforth she was going to devote her time to groups whose members paid a monthly fee for participation.

I attended three women's liberation conferences as well as weekly planning meetings to work out a conference that never took place. I also attended the 1973 NOW National Conference in Washington, D.C. Throughout the fieldwork period I went to feminist activities whenever possible: lectures, meetings, performances, fund-raising events. In addition, I took part in the formation of a Women's Caucus at the 1971 meeting of the American Anthropological Association. (During a meeting to initiate the caucus, a student remarked: "I don't want the caucus to work so that women can join the male hierarchy, I want to do things in a more female, you know, more egalitarian way." In my field notes, I wondered what she meant and noted that I had heard previous comments about the way women did things.)

I held informal interviews with feminists whenever possible, inquiring about life histories, feminist beliefs, and experiences. In April 1973 I interviewed a feminist about an abortion group then being investigated. My informant turned out to be exceptionally intelligent, articulate, and thoughtful, and I proposed the idea of following the movement career of one activist (see Appendix on p. 188). I taped an interview, collected further information during a subsequent interview, and showed the material to her at a later time. Although the project dealt with the informant's career in the women's movement, a great deal of personal information was offered spontaneously; this was presented with the movement data to illuminate feedback between the personal and the political.

I spent four weeks, in May and June 1973, collecting a list of as many Manhattan women's groupings as possible. This material helped me understand the multigroup structure of the movement.

In the spring of 1972 I prepared a written questionnaire for the university action group. The questionnaire was first given out at a group meeting, with additional copies distributed at subsequent meetings and work details. The unsigned responses of twenty-one participants were mailed back to me or left for me at the group's office.

Interaction was measured during the weekly meetings of the university group. I mapped where each woman sat, who volunteered to chair a meeting, who passed the agenda, and who wrote items on the agenda to be discussed. Unfortunately, it was impossible to measure informal interaction—who interrupted, who suggested compromises that were accepted, who talked for how long—without omitting the content of interaction; consequently, only formal actions were measured. These measures showed that, during a factional dispute between two influential women, when only one was present at a weekly meeting the majority of formal actions came from her half of the room. When she sat in the front, more actions were initiated in the front half; when she sat in the back, more actions were initiated in the back half of the room. During one meeting, with both women present, sitting one in the front and one in the back of the room, the same number of actions initiated by the same number of women came from each side—six actions were initiated by four women in the front, and six actions by four women in the back of the room. These interaction measures support my contention that, despite its ideology of leaderlessness, the university group did in fact have leaders.

During the fieldwork period I took part in women's liberation activities, attended NOW functions, interviewed women's suffragists, and lived the life of a Brooklyn Heights wife and mother. Different costumes were required for different activites, and I found that I was frequently carrying around a complete change of clothing: stockings, underwear, shoes, cosmetics, gloves, jewelry, blouse, skirt or jeans. I also discovered that a Brooklyn Heights matron was treated very differently from a women's liberationist—by outsiders and by movement women. Carden notes that she felt it would "violate her integrity" to dress differently from her usual pattern to interview women's liberationists. Consequently, she wore a dress, with somewhat different accessories, to interview both branches of the movement.[6] This sensible procedure had research implications, however, since her "rational" outfit placed Carden in a particular "moral" category for women's liberation participants. I was fortunate in having no difficulty in wearing the "uniform" (after having been alerted by a women's liberation classmate on appropriate dress): I owned and felt comfortable in jeans and boys' sneakers. I *was* unhappy about the fact that I didn't look very good in jeans. When I mentioned at a consciousness-raising group meeting that I just didn't seem to have the right shape for jeans, everyone laughed: "Oh, no one does!" One member then told me what store to visit and what brand to ask for in order to get jeans that fit properly. The necessity of dressing very differently for different occasions during a single day, the discovery that I behaved differently when dressed in different costumes, and was treated differently by onlookers, led to the thinking that culminated in chapter 6, on feminist demeanor and sexual deference.

Carden notes that she encountered different responses to her research from women's liberation and women's rights members. When women's rights members learned that she was a sociology professor writing a book about the movement, her research was accepted without question. Members of women's liberation, however, especially the more radical women, were less inclined to accept her academic credentials as a justification for her interest. Women's liberationists looked over Carden's shoulder, openly read her notes, criticized her research methodology, and chastised her for what were considered deceitful questions.[7]

I encountered no such difficulties. Three factors probably facilitated my research among women's liberationists: (1) my work was highly participative—I did not merely observe or interview, I took part in activities; (2) I looked, walked, talked, and frequently thought like a women's liberationist; and (3) I was a graduate student doing what was required of me to earn a degree, rather than a professor writing a book. I met only one objection to a research procedure during fieldwork. When my questionnaire was distributed at a weekly meeting of the university action group, one woman, who had come to the group for help in getting back her university job after being fired, objected that the information could be used against the group. A group activist, who was a graduate student in sociology, replied: "Look, we all know Joan, she's been part of the group for almost a year now. We've got to *help* other women with the things they're doing." Almost every woman present took a questionnaire, and the majority returned it filled out.

I followed women's movement literature as part of the research strategy. I regularly received and read nine feminist periodicals as well as feminist articles, pamphlets, newsletters, and books. Carden notes that a researcher must use movement literature with caution since it is generally produced by the most radical branches of feminism.[8] Although this makes the literature less representative of the views of the "average" feminist, the literature does represent feminist ideology and values, exemplifying the symbolism that pervades and defines the women's movement. Consequently, the fact that this material is extreme makes it particularly useful when investigating the political significance of symbolic beliefs and behaviors.

"The phone bill came today, didn't it?"

1

Becoming Sisters: Learning to Bond

1

What Is a Raised
Consciousness?

Central to contemporary feminism is the concept of a raised consciousness. The phrase is omnipresent in the women's movement: groups are formed for the purpose of consciousness raising; a woman may describe an experience, such as reading a book or having an abortion, that "instantly" raised her consciousness; individuals can be described in terms that suggest their consciousness is "low."

The phrase and its use suggest ascending levels:

> A woman in a consciousness-raising group described how her mother and aunts were really "down" during her adolescence. She made a stooping gesture with outstretched hand to illustrate their state. Her father had different dreams for her, though, and would tell how she was going to achieve something. But, after a brilliant college career, she went to a Freudian "shrink," who convinced her to get married, which she did. And she ended down, below, too. The stooping gesture was repeated.

In this instance the level referred to the informant's aspirations, which were raised by her father and lowered by the Freudian analyst. It also referred to the low social, emotional, and occupational position of her mother and aunts, and to her own position after marriage. It referred by implication to her present state. She had recently left her husband, after almost twenty years of marriage and three children, and joined a consciousness-raising group to try to "get her head together" and again raise the level of her aspirations and achievements.

A similar gesture was used by a lesbian feminist at a women's conference.

> In discussing her involvement with the women's movement, and self-development, she held her outstretched hand at waist level and said: "I used to be here. But I'm growing and changing and now I'm about here." Her hand went to chest level. "And I don't know *where* I'll be tomorrow!"

These ascending levels seemed to refer to this speaker's feelings of self-worth (she described how she gradually started to care less about how others conceptualized her and more about her own image of herself), to increasing feminist political activity (she was involved in organizing mass feminist demonstrations and small consciousness-raising groups), and to her attempt to achieve more meaningful and egalitarian relationships with other women.

"Consciousness" is by definition a subjective state. Raised consciousness can refer to becoming conscious of something one did not formerly perceive, of raising something from the unconscious to the conscious mind; to heightened consciousness of oneself or of a state of affairs; to an altered consciousness—to "having your head in a different place."

> A 48-year-old woman described her efforts to be independent and think independently since joining Older Women's Liberation. While undergoing a

personal crisis, however, she missed a number of group meetings and discovered that her old attitudes and behaviors were returning. "It's as if I have two heads," she said, "one a feminist head, the other, the old one, doing all the old things I used to do."

Having a "feminist head" clearly refers to the same constellation of subjective experiences as a "raised consciousness." The informant's statement suggests that in the process of getting a feminist head, individuals can alternate between high and low consciousness, between feminist and nonfeminist perceptions of reality.

It is worth noting here that the term "consciousness" is ambiguous, referring to a personal, subjective experience. This ambiguity may be a source of strength in the women's movement, where co-participants are able to agree that their consciousness is ascending, without the necessity to examine the possibly divergent contents of such individual consciousness. In a movement where participants may hold widely differing views, it is more unifying to discuss raised consciousness than to investigate the content of that consciousness.

The notion of ascending levels can provide a key to the meanings that cluster around this central, symbolic phrase. As indicated, these levels can refer to the social, economic, and emotional position of women, which is perceived as low, in need of being raised. It can also refer to women's perception of that inferior position, as well as to heightened (or raised) perception of the low position and of the urgency of the need to elevate it. Thus, the meanings center around an individual's (1) perception of women as a degraded group; (2) self-identification as a member of this group; and (3) commitment to personal or social change, or both, to elevate the position of women.

When a woman's consciousness is raised, she perceives herself and other women as members of a degraded group and is committed to altering this state. Such perception can be difficult. Many women find it intellectually and emotionally repugnant to define themselves as part of a low-status group composed of women, especially when alternative self-definitions based on social class, ethnicity, region, and religion are available. There may be additional difficulty in accepting the role of rebel against the status quo in order to elevate the position of women. The greatest difficulty is in *perceiving women as a group.*

Simmel discusses some problems of conceptualizing women as a group when each woman is integrated into an individual sphere, "prevented from transcending the group-relations established by marriage, family, social life." When women are seen as different from men, they must relate on unequal terms, and "the meaning of feminine existence lies exclusively in what the man cannot be or do, or does not want to be or do." When women have enough freedom so that they can display the qualities they hold in common with men, however, women can see themselves as a group, and be "conscious of their solidarity with all women." [1]

There is a cyclical quality to the history of the women's movement, and Simmel's formulation, first published in 1922, is relevant to the contemporary situation. For a woman to rupture or endanger what has been socially defined as primary ties—to family, husband, and social class—in order to perceive herself as a member of a new, and degraded, conceptual or interest group frequently requires an extraordinary and all-encompassing transformation in definition of self and of reality.

The concept of consciousness raising refers to such a transformation, where the individual "switches worlds." [2] Beliefs and behaviors that previously would have been inconceivable are now natural, indeed inevitable. Such revolutionary reality transformations occur through a process of resocialization, where the previous structure of reality is dismantled and meanings are radically reassigned. "Everything was turned upside down," said the woman describing the process by which the Freudian analyst had transformed aspirations so that marriage, rather than personal achievement, became her goal. She had been resocialized by the "shrink" and was again, after twenty years, three children, and an impending divorce, looking for a retransformed reality through the women's movement. Everything was to be turned upside down again—or right side up.

Berger and Luckmann point out that such reality transformations involve a new and effective "plausibility structure" presented by "significant others" with whom the individual identifies: "These significant others are the guides into the new reality."[3] Gerlach and Hine describe a similar phenomenon in their discussion of the "identity-altering" commitment process.[4]

A raised consciousness, then, refers to something close to a conversion experience. The significant others who introduce a woman to the transformed reality are her movement "sisters." * Involved in this "conversion" is a view of the individual's earlier life as preparation for the new reality, with the meaning of important people and events radically reinterpreted. Events are inserted or "remembered" when necessary to "harmonize the remembered with the reinterpreted past."[5]

When a woman's consciousness has been raised, she inhabits a transformed world in which her identity, biography, beliefs, and behavior have changed radically. She has become a feminist. She defines herself as a member of a group composed of women. She applies a "feminist analysis" to personal and political events. Indeed, personal events have *become* political; the private contents of the subjective female world—tenderness, love, sex, parent-child relations—are transformed into a political arena.

Such a transformation can be gradual or immediate, partial or almost total. Although a raised consciousness is a change in

---

* The term "sister" uses a kinship model, frequently employed by participants in social movements. It stresses what is perceived as previously neglected female linkages, between sisters, and between mothers and daughters, as opposed to the more frequent emphasis on links with men, with fathers, brothers, and husbands.

the head, a subjective change that in itself cannot be measured, it has ideological and behavioral consequences, many of which are visible and measurable. A woman with a feminist head talks differently, dresses differently, behaves differently. Her relationships with men and women have changed. Some of these "heavy changes" can be observed in the street, on the subway, in work situations; others are visible only in intimate situations—the intimacy of the consciousness-raising group, or that of the primary emotional relationships discussed in the consciousness-raising group.

One of the most important visible changes is in the extent of interaction with other movement participants. These are the significant others who form the community that defines and helps to maintain the "conversion." The more intense and exclusive the interaction, the deeper the commitment, with many feminists restricting significant interaction to other committed feminists.

The end point in a raised consciousness is a new and transformed world that displaces all previously inhabited worlds.[6] Part 1 examines the individual's journey toward sisterhood.

2

Beginnings

What makes a woman receptive to feminist ideas? And how does she get involved in the women's movement?

Certain life situations appear to increase receptivity, although as the movement develops through time, different people will be attracted for different reasons. During my fieldwork, from 1971 to 1973, the women's movement was not new, but it was young. To become involved, one did not have to confront the stigma and stereotypes applied to the feminists of the 1960s, but activists still faced some social and emotional risks. A woman no longer had to search to find a feminist group, but the movement was not yet socially acceptable; it took a sense of personal urgency or political commitment to provide the impetus for becoming involved.

Unlike contemporary feminists, the suffragists who won the vote for women in 1920 were reared in a feminist era. They did not have to transform their perceptions to become feminists because they grew up knowing what feminism was. As part of my fieldwork I interviewed fifteen women aged 77 to 91 who had worked for women's suffrage. (Eleven had worked for other causes as well; among them were peace, civil rights, birth control, and modern art.) It was difficult to learn exactly how and why these women had become interested in feminism sixty years ago. They made such statements as:

"I was born a suffragist, I think. I was born a feminist. I won't say suffragist—I was born a feminist!"

and

"I think all my life I believed in women's suffrage. . . . I just remember never thinking anything except that women have a right to vote and that it was curious that they didn't."

At the time these women became involved in the women's movement, just before World War I, a new and active surge of feminist activity was beginning, which culminated in the adoption of the suffragist amendment in 1920. Feminism was not new even then: there had been feminist activity since 1848; in fact, nine of the women I interviewed indicated that their mothers were feminists. One woman told with gentle humor of her Bryn Mawr education, directed by the redoubtable suffragist N. Carrie Thomas, and said of suffrage: "None of us could have depended on getting a degree if we hadn't cared about that!"

When asked when and how she and her lifelong friend and co-worker had been "converted" to suffrage, this woman replied:

"If you call it 'converted' . . . we rather assumed it. You see, so many things are in the misty past. We seem to have been completely ready for it."

I met no contemporary feminists who said their mothers had been feminists, although a number of women's liberationists described politically active mothers. Some said that they thought their mothers might have been feminists if there had been an active feminist movement when they were young adults. Although I found no "born feminists," I did find some who could perhaps be described as "natural activists." These women had become interested in feminism through political commitment. When women who were active in civil rights and New Left groups in the early 1960s decided that power and decision making were male prerogatives, with females relegated to food, typing, and sex, they directed their interest in liberation to a new group—their own. Stoloff found that significantly more women's liberation participants had a history of activity in radical politics than a matched group of nonactivist graduate students.[1] Her study utilized questionnaires, and did not explore why the women had moved from New Left politics to women's liberation. Nevertheless, a significant number of my informants mentioned dissatisfaction with the sexual division of labor in New Left groups as one reason they abandoned such groups for the women's movement.

> One woman told how she had become disillusioned with Students for a Democratic Society (SDS) in 1968, when she was organizing her women's college. "It wasn't even considered work by the men. Only what they did was important. . . . They did all the talking at the meetings. We felt we didn't know enough, and we thought if we worked very hard, then one day we might know enough to be able to talk at meetings too."

The rage directed at the *machismo* of New Left men by their former female colleagues is expressed by Morgan:

> Was it my brother who listed human beings among the *objects* which would be easily available after the Revolution: "Free grass, free food, free women, free acid, free clothes, etc.?" Was it my brother who wrote "Fuck your women till they can't stand up" and said that groupies were liberated chicks "cause they dug a

tit-shake instead of a hand-shake?" The epitome of female exclusionism—"men will make the Revolution—and their chicks." Not my brother, no. Not my revolution.[2]

In the late 1960s many such women shifted their field of activity to the women's liberation branch of the feminist movement. Some attempted to influence their organizations, forming women's caucuses or consciousness-raising groups; others moved from New Left to feminist organizations while retaining a Marxist orientation; still others decided that their primary commitment was to feminism.

In addition to the woman who is already politically oriented, other women are attracted to the movement for personal reasons, which later become reconceptualized as political. These women may not feel particularly receptive to feminism until they hear other women describe their experiences:

> At a meeting of female faculty called by a university women's liberation group, a number of women described underpaid and discriminatory job situations. One participant, a full professor of science who had been mentioned as a possible Nobel Award recipient, said nothing during the meeting. I was told afterward, however, that she had checked out the salaries in her own department and had discovered that younger and less respected men were earning more than she.

The discovery of job discrimination can be an important factor in sensitizing a woman to the movement. A female college graduate is offered a typist's job while male classmates are enrolled in executive training programs. A blue-collar woman discovers that she is a victim of discriminatory hiring practices or that on-the-job promotions are not available to her. Both are ripe for recruitment into feminist activity.

Before I examine more of the personal reasons for being attracted to the women's movement, let us discuss an extremely effective aspect of the social resistance to feminism. After the vote for women was won in 1920, the image of the suffragists became clouded. They were remembered as a group of half-demented, militant "old maid" battleaxes who sublimated their "feminine" impulses into an ill-advised and half-comic revolution. Ridicule had neutralized the threat posed by these women's abilities and achievements; the battleax image had transformed the suffragists into caricatures. Contemporary feminists have discovered with surprise that these women were revolutionary, articulate, intelligent, and very sane.

Similar tactics were used to belittle contemporary feminists.* In the 1960s a popular stereotype pictured women's movement participants as hysterical, shrill-voiced, physically blemished sexual and societal rejects. Women active in the movement at that time report that there were certain standard taunts from onlookers at feminist demonstrations: "You're ugly!" "What you need is a good fuck!" and "Lesbian!"

The women I worked with and observed over a period of two years were as attractive, intelligent, and well adjusted as the women I met in nonmovement circles. There was, of course, a fringe of disturbed individuals in the women's

---

* It is interesting to speculate why ridicule seems to be reserved for manifestations of the women's movement. Other social movements may be forgotten when they are in eclipse, but the participants are very seldom remembered as subjects for humor. Anarchists, for example, may be recalled as wild-eyed bomb-throwing "crazies," but perhaps they were a little too dangerous to be perceived as funny. And although onlookers may have been angered by the student and civil rights movements of the 1960s, I do not think their participants were regarded as objects of amusement. To give but one small example: would the people who so glibly discuss "women's lib" ever talk about "black pow"? Is there anything basically ridiculous about active, articulate women? Or is there something intrinsically threatening, which must therefore be minimized by ridicule?

movement (and out of it!), but I suspect that all social movements tend to attract a few such people. This problem was compounded in the women's movement, however, because participants were ideologically committed to "not putting another woman down" and consequently showed enormous patience and forbearance toward people who were clearly unbalanced.

Newton and Walton also take exception to the idea that "women's liberationists are misfits, failures, or ugly women who couldn't get a man." The seventeen women they interviewed at length seemed to be functioning adequately and on occasion outstandingly: "All the women were attractive in conventional terms, some exceptionally so," and no informants reported difficulty in attracting men.[3] Stoloff reports that the twenty-two women's liberation graduate students she surveyed tended to view themselves as more attractive to men than did the matched group of nonmovement counterparts; in addition, they had significantly more sexual encounters with men than the control group.[4] Gerlach and Hine were also unable to utilize criteria of social disorganization, deviance, or psychological maladjustment to differentiate participants from nonparticipants in the social movements they investigated.[5]

When society is conceptualized as a relatively homeostatic system, then any behavior attempting to generate far-reaching social and personal changes must by definition reflect social disorganization and/or individual maladjustment. If, on the other hand, we accept the view that individuals and roles do not always mesh with the social system, then we can accept the possibility that the system, rather than the individuals, requires change.

A number of personal stress situations can make a woman receptive to the movement, especially in large cities such as New York. Loneliness is one reason advanced by many first-time participants in women's movement activities. Interestingly, new participants describe their loneliness quite differently from veteran participants. Recruits are likely to discuss an unsatisfying relationship with a man, or no close relationships, as one reason they became interested in the movement. A recruit will describe a traumatic affair, disorientation following divorce or widowhood, or the feeling of being the only unpaired person in a world of couples. Women with previous movement experience, on the other hand, frequently explain attendance at movement activities in terms of wanting to meet new women friends.

Several factors make a woman particularly responsive to the movement following the loss of a marriage partner through divorce or death. For one thing, many women experience a pronounced loss of status when they are no longer one-half of a couple:

> "The higher you are, the farther you fall," said a woman in her 60s, describing the way her female friends gradually began to avoid her after the death of her husband, and how they seemed to fear any expression of interest or sympathy volunteered by their husbands. This woman introduced herself at a public feminist consciousness-raising session in terms of her husband's prestigious profession—despite the fact that he had been dead for more than a year.

A woman can feel she has lost her *identity* with the loss of a marriage partner. Berger and Luckmann discuss the way in which significant others can help an individual maintain or transform subjective reality.[6] A marriage partner can confirm a positive or negative identification from the outside world, or the spouse can disconfirm the world's identification, helping the individual maintain a desired subjective reality (or identity) despite contradictory messages from the rest of the world. In a troubled marriage, partners may confirm negative identities, and this negative identity may be a married woman's *only* identity, since she is less likely than her husband to have other identity-maintaining mechanisms available (an important job, a secretary, and so on). Thus the woman who loses a negative identity when she loses her husband may feel she has no identity at all.

At a feminist conference workshop, a just-assembled group of women discussed dependency. The topic was suggested by a participant who told how she had been divorced a year before, how she works at a relatively unsatisfying job, has two children and feels she is not living, but merely existing. It's as though she isn't there, she said. She finds it a feat to get through each day and more of a feat to get through the nights, even with sleeping medication. She wept as she spoke, and several women present started to cry. It was clear from the subsequent discussion that many of the women there had undergone similar experiences when their marriages broke up—even when they initiated the break.

In addition to loss of status, and perhaps identity, a woman who is no longer married is faced with a new personal and financial independence. If she went directly from her parents' to her husband's home, she may not know how to cope. Independence can be fraught with tension and financial hardship—especially in the case of contested divorces, which can be a nightmare to someone unused to decision making and calculated stress who is, in addition, financially dependent on the person she is struggling with.

A woman phoned the National Organization for Women (NOW) for help: She was calling from the Supreme Court building; her divorce suit had just been postponed for the third time; her husband had kidnapped her son while he was at camp and placed him in boarding school; the child had run away to her; the husband had given her no money for months and she was penniless, living at a women's hotel, and did not know where to put the son. The judge refused to listen; he had just postponed the case as her husband's lawyer suggested. The head of the NOW Committee on Marriage and Divorce was matter-of-fact when this was reported to her: "Oh, when they're into kidnapping, here's what you have to do . . ." she said.

Feminist organizations provide practical help and advice in such situations. In addition, female friendship and support can help a woman come to terms with her new status and altered role requirements. Women's movement participation provides a circle of sympathetic friends at the same time that movement ideology helps a woman define her changed role in positive terms of autonomy and independence, rather than in the more traditional terms of loss of comfort, status, even identity. A woman who receives help from a feminist group may stay with the group. She may then become active in helping others in similar situations. Among the functions performed by such aid is that of validating the changed identity of the helper.

Some women describe their movement participation in terms suggesting a sudden conversion.

"I always knew I *should* get into the movement," said one young woman. "I had this series of dead-end jobs. And I wasn't really satisfied with my life in any way. My relationships were dead-end too. And I knew, hearing about the movement from my friends and knowing I should do something. And then one day I just picked myself up and walked into the NOW office and volunteered to work, and I've been working there half-time ever since. I got myself a new part-time job, so I could live, and now the movement part of my life is the most important part."

Another informant told how she read *Sexual Politics* [7] and immediately phoned NOW and volunteered to work there.

"I've been there one day a week ever since," she said. "It's the only volunteer job I've ever held." She said she was not interested in a consciousness-raising group, the book raised her consciousness. She started to use her maiden name, although still married, and recently rebuked an executive who called her "dear." "There's no reason why he can't treat me as a person," she explained. "He wouldn't call a man 'dear.'"

Women who underwent traumatic illegal abortions are receptive to movement views on the subject as are those who have had easier abortions under movement auspices. Such women may later get involved in helping others who need abortions. Another pool of potential recruits is provided by women dissatisfied with the medical care they are receiving—especially from male doctors.

In life-crisis situations, the feminist view of reality helps a woman define what were previously believed to be personal difficulties as political problems shared by others. For example, Sarah Miller, a woman whose career in the women's movement was explored in depth (see Appendix), described how she became involved. Although highly trained, with a Ph.D. in cell biology, Sarah had stopped working to have children. In 1969 she was living in a sixth-floor tenement, with two children under the age of two, on her husband's salary of $4000 a year (as a New Left activist).

". . . my husband really didn't want to have anything to do with his family. He was not exactly thinking about leaving us, but he was having an affair with another woman, which I didn't know about at the time. He didn't want to have another child; it was me that wanted the second child. He didn't want to have anything to do with the one he had. He never did anything around the house. He never got up for the baby. He was out all the time. He was 100 percent involved in his work. And I couldn't count on him. So that I felt personally oppressed, in a way that I never had before."

This can be considered a life-crisis situation—a troubled marriage compounded by little money and the demands of two babies. In this situation Sarah, who confessed that she had always rather looked down on other women, gradually began to perceive herself as part of a group composed of women.

> "I had no friends in New York ... and I got to know my neighbors somewhat. I lived in a building with several young children, and we all helped each other out. And that was incredibly important to me. I could not possibly have survived without that. I came to depend on neighbors—women—in a very real way.... That experience made me identify with other women, ordinary women, in a way that—given my background—a lot of things probably wouldn't have."

The dissatisfaction with the status quo that may make women receptive to feminist ideology has frequently been crystallized by the movement itself. Without the women's movement the dissatisfaction that drives women to it might be vague, unfocused, or nonexistent.

Thus, Sarah Miller, dependent and isolated, had started to identify with other women—"ordinary women." But only after she attended a women's liberation conference and got to know feminists, who began to baby-sit for her ("Because of, you know, some notion of sisterhood") and criticize her husband because of his lack of participation, could she discuss her situation.

> "I began to be able, then, to tell a few people how unhappy I was, and how much ... I mean, up until that point, I refused to tell anyone anything about how bad the marriage was at that point. And I began to be able to tell people, and not feel that it was my fault."

Her new women's liberation friends probably had terms to describe the behavior of Sarah's husband: he was being "sexist" or "oppressive." Once the situation had a name, it could be perceived less as a personal flaw, about which to feel guilty, and more as a tangible situation shared by others. By naming a situation, a mood is formulated, and then mobilized by "making it a public possession, a social fact, rather than a set of disconnected, unrealized private emotions." [8]

Similarly, when Friedan sent a questionnaire to members of her Smith graduating class, she perceived a note of discontent that she called "the problem with no name." [9] When a problem with no name *is* named, and a book and numerous articles are devoted to it, the problem is not only discovered and defined but also in some ways created. Language has the power to "realize a world—not only to apprehend it but actually to produce the world." [10] A new way of categorizing reality not only names and channels dissatisfaction but also *generates* it.

When women become involved in the women's movement, and begin to perceive themselves as a group, then the groups with which they compare themselves change. They acquire a new "comparison group" [11] opposed to the group of women—men. When one's reference group changes, so does an individual's perception of a situation. What may have been previously satisfactory, or adequate, becomes unsatisfying and even unbearable.

Rather than grouping herself with husband, family, and social class, and comparing her group with like units, a woman who sees herself as part of a group called women may compare her circumstances with those of a man. Thus, when Sarah Miller began to identify with the other young housewives in her building, she began to see her situation as less satisfactory than that of her husband. Her situation may have been similar to that of many women she knew, but compared to a man of similar age and education, she was deprived. The situation has not necessarily changed; *what has changed is the reference point against which a person's situation is compared.*

The women's movement, then, helps actualize new expectations, in terms of which a woman feels deprived. This feeling of deprivation makes her more receptive to the movement. Reference points, or groups, that help shape reality are redefined; deprivation is experienced relative to these new reference points; and this deprivation can lead the person toward a stronger espousal of the new definition of reality.

Although receptive to the movement, Sarah Miller did not become involved until after she attended a women's liberation conference, where "everything the women's movement was trying to say somehow became clear." There are many such activities that attract new women. Movement groups sponsor film showings, conferences, rallies, debates. Many conferences consist of workshops run in consciousness-raising style; the women sit in a circle and take turns addressing themselves to a particular topic. The style of this public consciousness raising is intense and confessional; these sessions can be an overwhelming experience for novices, promising a new warmth, supportiveness, and sense of female community. Classes in women's studies may lead to further participation in the women's movement. Women's studies courses introduce a novice to new ideas and a new view of reality, to fellow students who may be movement activists, and to a teacher who may be perceived as the embodiment of female achievement. Together, the professor and her students are discovering the "real" history, psychology, sociology of women.

Possibly the most common way for a new woman to become involved in the movement is through a consciousness-raising group. Chapter 1 examined the phrase "raised consciousness." Now we will explore the dynamics of the consciousness-raising group.

3

Consciousness-raising Groups

Perhaps the most common introduction to the women's movement is joining a consciousness-raising group. For many women, this is their only exposure to the movement.

In the spring of 1972 one informant estimated that every block in Manhattan had at least one active consciousness-raising group. Observation tended to confirm this estimate. Consciousness raising seemed to be the fashion among middle-class women. This may have been part of a larger phenomenon. Small therapeutic groups were much in evidence at this time: encounter groups, sensory awareness groups, self-help groups of every persuasion and description.

There were a number of ways to find a consciousness-raising or "rap" group in New York City: through friends, a notice on the bulletin board of the Women's Liberation Center, public consciousness-raising sessions at feminist conferences where women looking for groups were introduced to one another afterward and encouraged to form their own groups, or the columns of the *Village Voice*. The New York Radical Feminists, Columbia Women's Liberation, and Older Women's Liberation had volunteers who answered telephone queries about consciousness raising: when they had a list of women from roughly the same area with the same night free, they would convene the group and, if the women wished, send an experienced volunteer to help the group get started. Older Women's Liberation and NOW had open public consciousness-raising sessions, as did WBAI, the FM radio station. The public NOW sessions were the only ones that admitted men and helped form consciousness-raising groups for men as well as women.

For a brief interval, people who called about consciousness raising were referred by NOW to a woman who ran "leadership training" consciousness-raising groups. This was the only consciousness raising with a leader I encountered during my fieldwork period; after 1972, NOW broke off with this "leader" when she began to charge for her services.

Let us start with a woman who wants to join a consciousness-raising group. Discontent or an acute life crisis are probably involved, even if that discontent was stimulated by the movement. Newton and Walton believe that discontent is a necessary but not sufficient condition for joining a consciousness-raising group; the majority of their informants described a personal contact as providing the final impetus.[1] The candidate may contact friends and start her own group or utilize one of the previously mentioned techniques for finding a group. At least one of the women involved in the new group is likely to have had some consciousness-raising experience, and a mimeographed guideline to forming and running groups is frequently in evidence.

Four to fifteen women may arrive at a prospective member's home. The women usually form a rough circle: consciousness-raising guidelines recommend this, and it is a fairly natural way to sit to be able to see everyone in the room. If a member of an established group or organization is helping, she may suggest the optimum number of participants (usually four to fifteen), meeting at someone's home, and the circle; she may also propose that novices go around the circle one at a time, giving brief biographies and telling why they wanted to join a group.

At the first meeting an introductory topic is selected.

Whether the first discussion is intensely personal or comparatively reserved probably depends less on the temperaments of participants than on previous movement (or psychotherapy) experience. Women with previous experience, or those desperate because of a personal crisis, can talk with devastating openness to a group of strangers.

Members frequently confess that the first meeting was unnerving. Problems of self-presentation arise. Those with previous movement experience have mastered the confessional mode, ritual phraseology, expected behaviors. Veterans discuss "forming a political community," the "oppression of women," and "how I was brainwashed" at the same time that novices talk of "girls" and are corrected—in the women's movement every female over grade-school age is a woman—and wait in vain for leadership, which more experienced participants do not provide as a matter of principle.

Some groups have a nucleus of experienced women whose verbal militancy may dismay a novice. Many women drop out or are in effect ejected from groups when they cannot accept the ideological assertion of the "oppression" of women.[2]

After two or three meetings, members have some sense of each other; faces acquire names, personalities, and brief histories. Every group has its own atmosphere, its own implied assumptions, its own modus operandi. After two to three months an extraordinary feeling of intimacy and trust can develop:

> "The loving stage. We were fascinated with each
> other. It was great for me; here all of the women were
> doing something with their lives.... We seemed to
> be peers. I felt really good."[3]

Eating together becomes significant; members may dine together before meetings or take turns bringing refreshments.[4] Women traditionally provide food for men and children, and sharing food among a group of women seems to have great symbolic meaning for members. This aspect of consciousness-raising groups was mentioned with great frequency by informants. Food becomes a multivalent symbol of nurturance, trust, of meeting physical and emotional needs, now available to women from women. (The slogan of a food-buying cooperative based at the New York Women's Liberation Center was "Women Feed Each Other.")

Confidences are shared at a deeper level than the first outpourings. Members learn one another's histories, and life crises are lived through by the group. The concern and support of the group extend to tangible measures: baby-sitting, co-signing a lease, legal aid. Members frequently start to meet outside the group: they will go to the movies or theater, initiate projects, borrow cars, share apartments. The group is now experienced as an organic entity, with members making a conscious attempt to verbalize resentments, to experience closeness and intimacy.

Naturally, intimacy is experienced only when a group is going well. A group can have an unsuccessful meeting; members may feel little was accomplished, or they may feel uncomfortable because hostility is manifested. Concealment of personal information, habitual lateness, or truancy can all cause hostility. When members are angry about another's behavior, they can confront the offender and attempt to solve the problem. One premise of interaction groups, whether therapy, encounter, or consciousness-raising, is that individuals have difficulty expressing displeasure; they suppress hostility, erupt in destructive anger, or discuss feelings behind the back of the instigator. The women's movement believes that men have been taught to handle and express anger while women must learn such techniques; one way to do so is in the supportive context of the consciousness-raising group.

When hostility is not confronted, a group can break up. Meetings become more tense, and the feeling of closeness vanishes. Members start to come later or to miss meetings. Meetings start at a later hour every week and often must be canceled at the last minute because too few members appear. A group may split into two, meeting separately; one faction may take over while dissidents leave; or members may gradually withdraw commitment and attendance as the group dies a slow death.

Informants report participation in a large number of groups that split up within three to six months. Sarah Miller, whose movement career was investigated, joined an unsuccessful consciousness-raising group that dissolved after four months, around the time she attended her first women's liberation conference. The following Christmas she joined a group that lasted for a year and a half. The seventeen women interviewed by Newton and Walton belonged to a total of twenty-eight consciousness-raising groups.[5] When a group splits, some members look for a new group, while others leave the movement permanently or temporarily. Because of the high mortality rate, new consciousness-raising groups frequently include women with previous experience—posing a problem if the veterans' consciousness is at a "higher" level than that of the novices.

Groups that break up during or before the "honeymoon" period of warmth and intimacy can be considered as having died prematurely. Those that survive have evolved techniques for dealing with tensions, venting hostility, expressing feelings directly, and eliciting such expression from more inhibited members. Informants describe a gradual progression in successful groups from superficial confessions and a rather abstract discussion of "society" and "the things it does to women" to an intense sharing of doubts, fears, discreditable incidents and sentiments in an atmosphere of support and trust.

To supplement this generalized discussion of the way consciousness-raising groups get started, let us examine the beginnings of a specific group.

CASE STUDY OF A CONSCIOUSNESS-RAISING GROUP

This group was a "spinoff" from a consciousness-raising group that had been meeting for a year and a half in the Washington Heights section of Manhattan. Women who inquired about consciousness raising were frequently referred to the Washington Heights group. Members received so many inquiries that they decided to pool the names so that a new group could be formed.

A list of applicants was given to one woman, who telephoned everyone and found six women, including herself, able to meet on Tuesday evenings. Inquiries about joining the Washington Heights group were initiated in the fall of 1971; the women who received the list started telephoning in January 1972; and the first meeting was held in early February 1972.

Five women attended the first meeting:

Rosa: 27, single, substitute teacher, Marxist, B.A. from City College, living with Sam, an unemployed artist. Grew up in the Bronx. Apartment on the upper West Side of Manhattan.

Jenny: 26, married four years, social worker, M.S.W. Hunter School of Social Work, husband a Ph.D. mathematician. Raised in the Bronx. Apartment in Washington Heights.

Susan: 23, single, on welfare, Bryn Mawr dropout, former SDS activist, lived in New Mexico commune, recently released from mental hospital where she underwent shock treatment. Raised in Westchester. Shared East Side Manhattan apartment with Nicola.

Nicola: 21, single, college student, enrolled in a welfare program that paid school fees and living expenses. Raised in the Bronx and Queens. Shared East Side Manhattan apartment with Susan.

Kate: 35, married, one child, student. Husband an executive of philanthropic foundation. Grew up in Brooklyn and Manhattan. Apartment in Greenwich Village.

The first meeting took place in Jenny's apartment. Her husband, who had been asked to go out for the evening, lingered to glimpse the women before leaving.

All the women were white, all came from middle-class

backgrounds, all were Jewish. This last fact was unplanned and was felt to be a source of embarrassment; members all said they wanted a more heterogeneous group. (Great amusement was occasioned at a later meeting when Nicola told how her boy friend had tried to denigrate the group by saying, "I bet all the women in your group are Jewish, between twenty and twenty-eight," and Nicola was able to reply triumphantly, "No, they are *not!*" Kate's age was the only factor that saved the group from this devastatingly accurate categorization.) No one had previous consciousness-raising experience, with the exception of Kate, who had belonged to a group that dissolved after three months. Four members had some psychotherapy experience, and Rosa, the fifth, said she was thinking of looking for a therapist. Four of the novices wore blue jeans; one, corduroy pants; four wore steel-rimmed glasses; three women wore men's workboots; two, women's leather boots. Cosmetics and bras were not in evidence.

The women decided to "just talk." The discussion was random, wide-ranging, and lively; Rosa, Jenny, Susan, and Nicola discovered they had friends in common and that the parents of Rosa, Nicola, and David (Jenny's husband) were old-line communists.

> Rosa, who had made the phone calls convening the group, spoke of her relationship with Sam, with whom she was living, of the Manhattan commune in which they had lived before Sam had a fight and left, and of an earlier trip to California the two had taken.
>
> Jenny described her new job as a social worker, which she liked, and told how she and her husband were the only people they knew who worked full-time; she said that since our society liked tall, thin people and she was tall and thin, she was satisfied with her body. She said little about her husband, except to comment that men and women seemed to have a lot of fantasies about each other, and that she had a lot of fantasies.

Kate told how she had gone back to college and liked it, of how her previous consciousness-raising group had broken up, and how she wanted a group where there were women with children so she could discuss some of her problems as a married student with a child.

Nicola said she had just had an abortion, her second, from the same relationship, now ended, and told how that affair had started: She was introduced to her lover by another man who fell in love with her on sight when they were fourteen; but the man who introduced them was also in love with his best friend, Patrick, and when she and Patrick met and started going together, the man who introduced them almost killed himself, and talked of shooting the two of them. Nicola talked more than the others; she discussed her life as though recounting a soap opera about someone else.

Susan told of the New Mexico commune she lived in for two years where she was "very much into gardening and making adobe bricks," of how she "flipped out" and left the commune, returning home, where her parents committed her to a psychiatric hospital. She later discovered she had had a fantasy about the man she had been in the commune with, and he about her; they hadn't been real people but fantasies to each other.

The women decided they liked one another enough to keep on meeting; the next meeting was planned for the following week at the apartment shared by Nicola and Susan. The subject to be discussed would be mothers.

The following Tuesday evening Kate was out of town and Jenny stayed home with a toothache. The three women who met decided there were too few members present and canceled the meeting. The following week members agreed to try not to miss meetings and to give as much advance notice as possible when absence was unavoidable.

The third meeting was held at the Washington Heights home of Ruth, one of the original list of applicants. Ruth had subsequently joined another consciousness-raising group, but wanted to meet this group; members were eager to have Ruth because she would diversify their membership. Ruth was twenty-six, divorced with two children, and a substitute teacher. She had a B.A. from Hunter College and had been raised in the Bronx. Ruth wore blue jeans, a T-shirt with no bra, steel-rimmed glasses, men's workboots, and no cosmetics; she had a rumpled, curly noncoiffure resembling that of Jenny and Susan.

> Ruth told how she had met her husband as an undergraduate when he was teaching at Hunter; how she had married at graduation and had a child "nine months and a day" after marrying; of how her husband was a natural student who switched fields when close to a Ph.D., but she got bored and lonely and wanted gaiety. She said she had a boy friend who was good to the children and wanted to marry her, but she'd like to date and have fun and not get tied down again just yet.

The women discussed their mothers but got sidetracked into biographical details. The women seemed to shift very easily from discussing their mothers to discussing themselves, as though the boundaries between themselves and their mothers were hazy and indefinite.

> Kate talked about the demands of her duplex apartment, and of her husband who did much business entertaining, and voiced fears that the other women would dislike her when they saw her life style, which was more elaborate than theirs.
>
> Rosa spoke of her intermittent relationship with Sam, telling how difficult he was, and describing their trip to Los Angeles two years before, after he had left his wife.

Jenny said she intended to adopt a child when she was about thirty-five, since she thought having kids could be such an "ego trip," and wondered why she had gotten married rather than merely living with her husband. She said that if her marriage broke up, she wasn't sure she'd bother to marry again.

Nicola told more about her relationship with Patrick, a musician who earned a living by "dealing" [marijuana], and who blackened her eye once when she said she wanted to leave him.

Susan described how she and Jim had lived on a school bus and in a commune together; she said it was a real "fantasy trip"—she was his squaw—they both felt not being able to adjust to the straight world made them so great and far out; they were both into really heavy drugs, LSD and peyote, until she flipped out and came home. She described the hospital and shock treatment, and told how Jim had come to get her—it was really romantic, "like a knight or something."

The women decided to meet at Kate's apartment the following week, after Kate exacted an agreement that they would not all "hate her" when they saw her well-furnished duplex. The new woman, Ruth, said she would stay with her first consciousness-raising group because she could not afford sitters to attend both groups.

The following week the members discussed the same topic—mothers. The other women questioned Kate about her relationship with her ten-year-old daughter; they seemed intrigued by a view of the mother-daughter relationship from the mother's side.

Jenny mentioned, for the second time, her desire to live in a commune, but said her husband was set in his new college teaching job and in four-times-weekly psychoanalysis; she said she would probably have to leave David if she were serious about a commune; she touched again on her active fantasy life; but did not discuss the contents of these fantasies.

Kate suggested that, since her Greenwich Village apartment was easily reached by the others and she was the only member who had to hire a sitter to attend meetings, the group meet at her place for a time. The others assented.

The next week the women all confessed they had found the previous meeting unsatisfying. They decided the discussion had been too abstract, that they had discussed other people's ideas and experiences, and they agreed now to try to talk only about their own personal experiences and feelings. They also decided to go around in a circle, taking turns speaking. The subject of lateness was raised—Nicola had been thirty minutes late to every meeting—and the group decided to start half an hour later, with every member promising to try to arrive on time. Jenny wondered if some of the feeling of discomfort the previous week resulted from the fact that everyone was so down on mothers and Kate was a mother. This was discussed, as was the prearranged subject—why members had come to the group and what each wanted from women's liberation. The women discovered that each wanted to learn how to react effectively when she encountered "put downs" of women; every member felt she had difficulty expressing anger and all wanted to learn how to get angry without losing control. "I always smile when I feel furious or else I get mad and yell, or cry," said Nicola. The others assented. They agreed that men appeared to know how to express disapproval and anger, and decided they would try to develop this ability.

Kate still wanted additional married members with children. Nicola knew another consciousness-raising group that had several members with children; the group discussed the possibility of merging with them and decided to have a joint meeting the following week. Kate served coffee, cake, and soda, and they all agreed that it had been a very good meeting. The women sat together, eating, drinking, and gossiping until midnight. There was an atmosphere of closeness and warmth.

To explore the possibilities of merging groups, a meeting with the second consciousness-raising group was scheduled for the following week. The five members of the first group came to Kate's, as did a new applicant—Sandy, a friend of Jenny's, who had expressed interest a few weeks earlier. So did seven members of the second consciousness-raising group, making thirteen women in all. The new group was older, with members aged twenty-seven to forty-five; four of the seven women had children, ranging from ten months to sixteen years old. There was no prearranged topic, and the conversation skipped from subject to subject.

Members of each group sat together until Nicola suggested they shift places. The new women talked about "sexism," about the way society "brainwashes" and "breaks the will" of women, of the "male chauvinism" and "oppression" they encountered. None of these terms had come up in the first group. Members of the first group were all somewhat receptive to a psychoanalytic view of behavior; this was expressed in an assumption that it was important to explore what women did to get *themselves* into trouble. This orientation was met with hostility by the new group, which focused entirely on what society did to women. It was clear that the second group considered "shrinks" the enemy; they appeared to take it for granted that psychotherapists were agents of a malevolent society whose sole function was to socialize women into unsatisfying and inferior roles.

There was a sense of polarization, of *we* and *they*. Even Sandy, the new member, was swept into the unity of the first group. Two women from the second group, both in their mid-forties, interrupted discussions, contradicted statements, and talked to one another as others spoke; this was met by significant glances, raised eyebrows, and looks of sympathy among members of the first group. At the end of the meeting the women discussed where to meet the following week. Kate offered her apartment again. This was strongly objected to by the two older women, who said it was a matter of principle that the group meet at different places. No one could agree upon an alternative place, however, and both groups reluctantly decided to meet at Kate's again.

Throughout the following week there were telephone calls between members of the first group; everyone had wanted to stay behind to discuss the "bad vibes" at the meeting. Nicola thought the new women had been intimidated by Kate's well-furnished duplex apartment: "You know, we all rapped about it before we came, they just walked in." Jenny was exasperated by the second group's insistence on blaming all difficulties on society: "It's as though they have nothing to do with what happens to them," she complained.

A few hours before the second joint meeting, a member of the second group telephoned Kate; they had decided they would rather meet separately and not merge groups. The decision was greeted with relief by members of the first group. Even Kate agreed to give up her demand for more women with children. The women stood in Kate's kitchen, stuffing themselves with cake and soda, laughing, gossiping, and waiting for the coffee to perk. Although it was only her second meeting, Sandy, Jenny's friend, seemed to be part of the group. Sandy was twenty-eight, a divorced medical student with a B.A. from the University of Michigan. She had grown up in the Bronx and had an apartment on the lower East Side of Manhattan.

The women moved into the living room, with the remaining food, and the meeting began.

> Rosa, who had just left Sam and moved into her own apartment, told how pleasant it was not to have to cook for someone else. Somehow she had started taking care of meals and housework when she and Sam were both working: Sam claimed she worked shorter hours, and later, when he was unemployed, he said she made enough money for both to live on, but even then he didn't really help much around the house.

> Jenny said she had stopped making a big thing about meals. When the group first started, she used to rush home from work and leave a big dinner waiting for

her husband; now she goes to consciousness-raising meetings and to evening karate classes, and David can get his own meals or eat out if he's hungry. She's stopped being so uptight about meals and worrying hours ahead about what's for dinner; David can worry too, she said, or go hungry.

Susan told how she and another woman somehow found they had responsibility for meals at the commune—if they didn't do it there just wasn't anything to eat and thirty people went hungry. "Someone has to start worrying and planning early in the day about what you're going to eat," she said, "and it always seemed to be us."

Jenny wondered why she and the others took responsibility for a proper meal only with or for a man. "No wonder all those people who get married get fat," she declared, "all those three-course meals all of a sudden!"

Sandy inquired why women don't prepare really good meals for other women. "Do you only become a grown-up with grown-up meals when you get married, with wedding presents—china, dishes and all that?" she asked. She had an unmarried female professor at medical school who invited her to dinner and served a beautiful meal on proper dishes and everything. Why should all that fuss only be for men?

Kate talked about her household responsibilities and conflicts between family and schoolwork, and told how her husband, who frequently works late, suggested she leave their 10-year-old daughter alone in the apartment one evening when she had to go to the library for an important school project, and how she had felt worried and guilty about the child's welfare and had consequently stayed home.

Jenny suggested that Kate ask her daughter how she would have felt at being left alone. "You have to change constantly to be a parent," she said reflectively. "Perhaps you have to change, Kate, and learn to leave your daughter alone."

The group had been meeting for two months by this time, and a feeling of relaxation and trust was growing. Kate had been serving coffee and soda; the others decided to take turns bringing food. Members felt the group was an organic entity; all were committed to attending meetings regularly, arriving on time, and attempting to draw out less verbal women. Nicola and Kate, who talked more than the others, both made an effort to speak less and to make sure everyone had a turn to speak. In subsequent meetings the group discussed feelings about having children—there seemed to be some fear of what was seen as a definitive commitment to an adult role; their relations with women friends—almost every member said she would like to learn to relate to women more closely and honestly; and how relationships with men affected relationships with women.

During this time Jenny confessed that she had been having an extramarital affair for a year; she felt she had no one to discuss this with safely and wanted to talk about it with the group; she expressed ambivalent feelings for both husband and lover. In the spring Sandy's new lover, the first man she had dated since her divorce two years before, was killed—shot by a police bullet, as a bystander during a holdup. The group offered emotional support and tangible help: when Jenny eventually decided to leave her husband, she moved in with Nicola and Susan while apartment-hunting; members offered to baby-sit for Kate during school emergencies; and all the women spent time with Sandy, after the death of her lover, when she did not want to be alone.

At the last meeting in June, before the group recessed for the summer, the women dined together at a restaurant. Before parting, Nicola said with the approval of the others, "Next September, I think we should take turns meeting at everyone's place; we can pay for a baby-sitter for Kate." This was an acknowledgment that, although Kate was older and better established, the group had achieved a dynamic balance, with every member ready to contribute as much as she could.

This case study has examined the first five months of one consciousness-raising group (which continued to meet throughout the following year). The group was less militant than many; only one member had previous consciousness-raising experience; there were no movement activists in the group; members were concerned with the individual's—as well as society's—role in lack of self-actualization; and all members were committed to heterosexual love although a few had experimented with brief homosexual activity.

Members never discussed "brainwashing" or "oppression" in so many words. They did, however, move toward a sense of commonality in feelings and experiences; every woman wanted to learn to express anger more effectively; members began to question the automatic female assumption of domestic responsibility and explore ways of relinquishing or not assuming sole responsibility for home and meals; and members, after examining competitive feelings toward women, began to express a growing feeling of closeness to one another and to other women. The women discovered a common pattern in relationships with women friends, where close female friends were abandoned when an affair with a man was initiated. Frequently all other relationships had been ignored in favor of an intense and exclusive concentration upon the "beloved." Discussion revealed that such relationships generally ended badly: one member had an abortion, another a psychiatric illness near the end of such an affair. The women decided that "love-as-a-solution" seemed to place intolerable burdens on a relationship, and that one of these burdens was an unthinking severance of ties with women. Members expressed sorrow and guilt about what was retrospectively perceived as betrayal of a close female friend. Incidents related included initiation of an affair with the older brother of a best friend, breaking up the friendship; the attraction and eventual annexation of the man a friend was interested in; and the involving of a dependent and troubled (and, possibly, lesbian) friend in sex *à trois* with the narrator and a man. With the exception of one woman, who had kept the friends of her childhood through marriage, members described long-term intermittent friendships with women interrupted by intense, and most frequently, short-term relationships with men.

The fact that relationships with women were given as much importance in discussion as those with men—as though it were possible to fail in a relationship with a woman as well as a man—was in itself a learning experience to these women, who had previously assumed that female friendship was less meaningful, serving as a time-filler for life spaces between men. The lower value placed on friendship with women was questioned, not only through discussion of past incidents, but also through the growing importance of group members to one another. Members found they were reordering priorities, placing the group meeting before appointments with men. This bonding between women evoked resentment, hostility, or ridicule from husbands and lovers, who appeared to perceive women in a group as a threat. (The most positive male reaction reported was an uneasy and often reiterated, "What do you *talk* about with them?") Members learned to feel close, to trust one another. The group experience of intimacy was extended to other women; each member reported she was beginning to feel more open with women, to find women more interesting and less threatening.

The women in the case study learned to be intimate with other women in the consciousness-raising group. I believe that teaching women to *bond* is the single most important function of such a group. Feminist articles and guidelines on consciousness raising mention a number of group goals. These have a common core involving intimacy and support; a feeling of belonging to the small female group and, by extension, to a larger group, composed of women; a gradual awareness that this larger group is degraded or oppressed; and some commitment to personal and/or social change. In short, consciousness-raising groups help the individual perceive herself as a member of a group composed of women. Central to this raising of consciousness is the experience of intimacy and trust between women in the small group.

Although women in a consciousness-raising group share a commitment to personal change, to defining and achieving a more satisfactory life pattern, commitment is not the same as actual change. Do changes occur? Here, an interesting paradox is found. For some women the consciousness-raising group seems to act as a matrix for wide-ranging personal changes. For others, however, the group appears to function as a safety valve, allowing hostility and resentment to be vented without threatening the participant's life outside the group. The group, then, helps some women change, while helping others *not* to change.

> One consciousness-raising group spent much time discussing a classic feminist argument over who will do the housework.[6] One member, with two young children, expressed resentment against her husband, who had told her to "stop bitching and go out and get a job if that's what you want." Although the husband, who taught two days a week and was home writing his Ph.D. dissertation the rest of the time, helped her, she complained that she had primary responsibility for the children and household and that he did not understand the difficulties of her position. This woman talked of going back to school, of getting a part-time job, of taking a full-time job, of somehow escaping an exclusive preoccupation with household and children; but she did nothing to change her situation. In fact, when her husband walked out, all her efforts were directed at getting him back, with no attempt to change her household situation in any way. This young woman may well have been a victim of society in her paralysis of will and inability to initiate wished-for life changes.[7] The consciousness-raising group may have helped to reinforce this paralysis, however, by giving her an outlet

for verbally venting her feelings, thus, possibly, diminishing pressure for behavioral changes. Verbally this woman was a militant feminist, but she did nothing to change her life.

And again:

A male informant told me that the most "gung-ho" feminists in his wife's consciousness-raising group were those with the most oppressive (and unchanging) outside lives.

Is it possible to identify women most likely to use a consciousness-raising group to help them resist, rather than initiate, behavioral changes? One group in particular uses consciousness-raising groups as a safety valve, to help preserve the status quo—married women with young children. This is probably related to the difficulty of going it alone with young children, and to the comparatively temporary nature of the predicament.

Thus, many women will not leave a marriage with young children, knowing that the alternative may be intense financial and emotional deprivation. No women's movement institutions exist that offer the same financial and emotional support for women with children as does married heterosexuality.[8] Some women may not wish to change their situation, even if it is felt to be unsatisfactory, because the alternatives are perceived as worse.

In addition, middle-class women at home with young children may believe that the most difficult stage is temporary, that infants and toddlers eventually go to school, ending the mother's confinement to a world of women and young children and freeing her for alternate uses of her time. Women with professional aspirations are frequently in a double-bind situation: they may have chosen to stay with their children, at least for a time, believing they have more to offer the children than a mother-substitute; yet they are constantly reminded that child care has little prestige compared to professional advancement—advancement jeopardized by the time devoted to children rather than to a career. Although temporary, the situation may be experienced as intolerable. A consciousness-raising group helps such a woman express anger at her husband—who is perceived as benefiting from the joys of family while achieving professional satisfaction—and at "the system" that places her in the double-bind.

Two groups of married women with young children are under discussion, with some possible overlap. Women in both groups may feel dissatisfaction with their marriages. But for one group the disquiet may be relatively temporary, easing when the children go to school; for the second, the malaise may be more permanent, although the women are afraid to break up the marriages because of the difficulties of rearing children alone.

In each case a consciousness-raising group can help women let off steam verbally without making revolutionary behavioral changes that might threaten the status quo—a status quo that may be seen as unsatisfactory, but to which no better alternatives are presented.

Perhaps there has been a suggestion of a dividing line, which classifies marriages as satisfactory or unsatisfactory. This is an oversimplification. It is more productive to view marriage as an ongoing *process*, which demands commitment to spouse, to children if they are present, and to the institution itself. Commitment may well be finite, with the relationship between the woman, her marriage, and the women's movement resembling a zero-sum game; when more commitment is expanded in one area, it decreases in another. In this view increased commitment to the movement and, consequently, to women as a group or class will threaten a marriage; continuing commitment to the marriage (and conceivably to heterosexual relations) will leave a limited sum of emotional energy to be expended on the movement.

This examination started with a hypothetical woman who

finds and joins a consciousness-raising group. If the group survives, our hypothetical member will have acquired a raised consciousness. This will involve cognitive, interpersonal, and possibly behavioral changes. Now, let us explore some of the "heavy changes" a woman goes through while "getting a feminist head."

What Happens to Groups When
Consciousness Is Raised?

Many consciousness-raising groups have no formal affiliation with other women's movement organizations. When members feel that such groups have fulfilled their function of facilitating personal change, the fate of the group is in doubt. Many groups break up at this time, while others look for a new project or function. Some groups undertake political action, by helping other consciousness-raising groups get started; members may help form new groups as well as publishing articles and guidelines on consciousness raising.

In 1969 the New York Radical Feminists tried to solve the problem of transition from small, isolated consciousness-raising groups devoted primarily to personal change to a mass movement working for social change. This involved a three-stage process:
1. A small group moved from consciousness raising to reading movement literature.
2. At an optional second stage the group could apply to join the Radical Feminist organization.
3. At a final stage, the group would have full autonomy to undertake political actions.

The plan floundered, however, and the Radical Feminists—and indeed the women's movement as a whole—have no formal structure today that guides groups from consciousness raising to political action.

Some consciousness-raising groups get involved in action projects, and some are devoted to both consciousness raising and action from the beginning. Others, organized by or affiliated with action groups, serve as a source of potential recruits for the "mother" group. The transition from individual to social change is not automatic, however, and many consciousness-raising groups dissolve, leaving members with no ties to the women's movement. Such women may define themselves as members of an informal interest group composed of women, but they have no ties to an organized grouping.

4

Altered Relationships with Women and Men

One of the most striking changes reported by informants as a result of a raised consciousness occurs in relationships with other women.

Women in our society tend to perceive other women as competitors—for men. This begins early. A ten-year-old girl said of her sixth-grade class: "The boys all stick together, the girls doublecross each other." A woman in her thirties wrote:

> Men compete for rewards and achievements. We compete for men. Men vie for worldly approval and status. We vie for husbands. Men measure themselves against standards of excellence and an established level of performance. We measure ourselves against one another.[1]

Such behavior has been variously explained by biology, psychology, and culture. Lionel Tiger attributes male bonding to a primate "biogram," with women competing for high-status bonded males; Freud endows women with "little sense of justice . . . no doubt related to the predominance of envy in their mental life"; and feminists point out that women are socialized to be passive and dependent, to express aggression against safe targets—other women—and to measure their worth by the response of others.[2] Married women in our society tend to group themselves with husband and family, separate from other women and their families. Simmel, who notes this, sees the isolation as a cultural product.[3]

A central function of consciousness-raising groups is teaching women to be intimate with other women. Women who have learned in consciousness raising to feel relaxed and easy with other women find that this ease extends to women outside the consciousness-raising group; for example, they find that they no longer concentrate exclusively on men at parties. When the barriers of competitiveness and distrust are down, women discover that they have much to say to one another. Naturally, not only feminists talk to other women. There are, however, certain stereotyped female topics— fashion, cosmetics, home furnishing, cooking, child care—that allow women to converse with minimal communication effected. These are "safe" topics; the speaker is free to reveal as little of herself as she wishes. Although many women find such "feminine" subjects engrossing, when such conversation is used as a defensive shield, to conceal rather than communicate, it can bore participants, who may then conclude that men are more interesting.

Women with successful consciousness-raising group experience frequently extend the trust gained there to other women. With less defensive conversation, more communication is possible, especially since consciousness raising has given a member a rich repertoire of engrossing topics: How do you feel about your body? Do the men at your job look at you as though . . . ? When your kids cry when you want to do something interesting, what do you do? Don't you hate it when men say . . . ?

The consciousness-raising confessional mode has its (unspoken) conventions, as does the "feminine" or little-woman mode. In consciousness raising one confesses financial problems, but conceals the lack of them—financial ease is middle class and vaguely discreditable. One reveals difficulties or disillusion with men, but says little about good relationships with the opposite sex—a good relationship is a personal, or private, solution and politically somewhat suspect unless it involves political solutions such as sharing the housework. One discusses one's work, but keeps discreetly quiet about the joys of motherhood—although one is free to describe the difficulties and inconveniences posed by children. There is, in short, an inversion of the conventions of middle-class female conversation, where consumption is stressed, financial and marital difficulties glossed over, and motherhood glorified.

Informants report a change in feelings about mothers as they start to feel closer to women. Novices frequently express negative perceptions of their mothers in consciousness raising; mothers are described as boring housewives, dependent wives, manipulative parents. The mother is depicted as less independent, less interesting, less *human* than the father, who is envied even when resented. High school and college students say their mothers had unsatisfying lives, and describe attempts by the mother to relive life through her daughter, pushing the daughter toward sexual popularity and/or academic and professional achievement. Women in their twenties often discuss the limits between mother and daughter in hazy and indefinite terms, as though the narrator had difficulty knowing where her mother left off and she, herself, began. The mother appears to be perceived as part of the daughter; or the daughter seems to feel she is part of the mother. The mother is also described as the daughter's fate— an inferior fate. The father, on the other hand, is frequently described in potent and instrumental terms even when these terms are negative. As women's consciousness is raised, "society" or "the system" is gradually defined as the enemy, with both mother and daughter as victims. The mother's child-rearing practices, her clinging and manipulative behavior, are perceived as reactions to a feeling of personal powerlessness, a feeling shared by the daughter. When the daughter redefines herself as a victim of society and redefines her goals to include challenging this victimization, her relationship with her mother is also redefined. She no longer perceives herself as her mother's victim. Instead, the daughter, who in her search for independence frequently identified with the father as an embodiment of autonomy, now identifies with the mother; mother and daughter are deprived of independence by the father and by society. One woman discussed changes in perception due to consciousness raising.

> "I am much, much more sympathetic with my mother. I have much more admiration for her because she was very much before her time in ways—very self-reliant and rebellious.... I have much less respect for my father than I had and am more aware of his contemptuous and hateful feelings toward women and how he played these feelings out on my mother." [4]

What were originally defined as personal problems between mother and daughter are now seen as a shared social problem, responsive to political rather than interpersonal solutions.

A woman who becomes active in the women's movement does not only feel closer to women but also spends more time with them. If her consciousness-raising group is meeting, one night a week is devoted to it. If she belongs to an action group, it will probably meet weekly as well. When the action group plans projects, there will be special projects and meetings. The new feminist has made new female friends. They attend feminist films, conferences, forums, restaurants. Feminist conferences are most frequently scheduled for weekends and holidays. With the exception of NOW functions, where men are welcomed, these activities are generally restricted to women. A woman can be busy with movement activities every night, holiday, and weekend if she so desires. With raised consciousness, time with women is not seen as second best; it has been chosen.

Women are beginning to value women more. Obviously they are no longer as concerned with male approval, particularly when that approval conflicts with their own growth. . . . Once women decide to *choose* the company of women, the women's groups they enter take on a *valued status* as a preferred activity.[5]

New feminists, then, start to like women more and to spend more time with them. At the same time they may feel dissatisfied with, or angry at, men. Women who discover in a consciousness-raising group, for example, that "painful personal problems are common to many of the women present," may stop blaming themselves for these problems.[6] Someone who has been taking the blame for interpersonal problems in a relationship, and abruptly ceases to do so, changes the balance of that relationship. A behavioral change so small as a refusal to cry, with the woman quietly holding her ground during a disagreement, supported in the background by her consciousness-raising group, with whom she has discussed the problem, can change the dynamics of a relationship.

In a feminist conference workshop on Marriage and the Family, one woman told how she had stopped feeling guilty and acting ingratiating every time her husband of eighteen years became moody. When she no longer reacted to his moods, he became much easier to live with, she reported. She said her consciousness-raising group had helped her develop a stronger sense of herself; without this, she believed she would not have been able to stop interacting with her husband in this self-destructive manner. Two other women in the room reported similar experiences. One said of the improved relationship: "I was no longer the victim."

A relationship can change when a woman stops taking the

blame. But many women go one step further: not only do they refuse the blame, *they assign it to their men.* It can be a heady experience to stop feeling inferior, dependent, unable to exist without masculine companionship and support. With this feeling of liberation, of new emotional energy, comes anger; a woman begins to feel angry about the past, when she in retrospect believes that she unfairly took the blame, knuckled under because of weakness, and suppressed her own interests and abilities to nurture those of her husband or lover. Although this anger may be expressed in terms of tangible events, it has a volcanic quality. Anger is not so much expressed as it erupts, as though it had been simmering below the surface for years. Women report that, suddenly, they are furious at construction workers.

> They did their usual number and I was not really surprised, but I reacted more intensely than I ever had before, reacted so intensely that it shocked even me. I gave them the finger and had a fantasy about ramming that finger up the most well-shaped ass around, ramming it so hard that he would fly up into the scaffolding. . . .[7]

They find themselves turning in pure rage on men who have made comparatively innocuous remarks about "the way women are." This anger may permeate a love affair or marriage. Many relationships with men become troubled at this stage—because a woman overreacts to a remark or incident, seeing it as representative of what is now interpreted as months or years of "oppression." Or because an angry woman is not easy to be with, or live with. Or because a man has become used to a complaisant, dependent woman and refuses to accept change. Or because a certain elasticity, necessary in human relationships, where each person must give as well as take, cannot exist side by side with once-buried anger that is suddenly erupting.

The release of anger and new demands that frequently

accompany a raised consciousness seem to place an almost intolerable burden upon existing male-female relationships. Some survive on a new basis:

> "When we started living with each other I used to cook every night and laugh at all of his jokes. . . . But we've really worked out all of those blindnesses and it wasn't easy, but some of it was really a lot of fun and I'm glad we did it. We wouldn't have the understanding of each other today if we hadn't been through this. We split everything down the middle."

And others continue with increased strains:

> "My husband still wants me to organize myself around his needs. . . . It's still a power struggle. He does some things, but not as much as he should. My husband has been inconvenienced by my liberation, although he liked it intellectually. He became more and more hostile to the women in my life. . . . I don't know if our relationship can survive, I feel cheated. If my marriage breaks up, I'll never marry again." [8]

Many heterosexual relationships dissolve under the pressure of anger and increased female expectations. It is possible that expectations for happiness, fulfillment, for personal growth and autonomy cannot be filled by marriage or, indeed, by any interpersonal relationship. But in the women's movement, and in consciousness raising in particular, women who have suddenly raised their expectations may place the burden of lack of growth and fulfillment, of frustration, upon husbands and lovers.

The support of a consciousness-raising group can facilitate blaming the man in one's life. Group members become the significant others that validate reality, replacing the nuclear family unit or love relationship. The woman is free to construct a new definition of reality, validate it with the consciousness-raising group, and work out the implications of this new definition in the interpersonal arena.

Berger and Kellner examine the function of marriage in our society "as a social arrangement that creates for the individual the sort of order in which he can experience his life as making sense."[9] They believe that a private sphere of existence has been separated from public life at the same time that this sphere has been defined as the principal area for an individual's self-realization.

> Every individual requires the ongoing validation of his world, including crucially the validation of his identity and place in this world, by those few who are his truly significant others. Just as the individual's deprivation of relationship with his significant others will plunge him into anomia, so their continued presence will sustain for him that *nomos* by which he can feel at home in the world at least most of the time.[10]

The authors believe that marriage fills this world-building function in modern industrial society and that this function is reflected and reinforced by a familistic ideology. When love relationships are seen as a preparation or substitute for marriage, they too are expected to fulfill this world-building function.

There are a number of possible consequences when the consciousness-raising group replaces love affairs or marriage in validating reality. First, quite simply, the group offers companionship, which can decrease pressure toward heterosexual activity merely for the sake of "not being alone." A member who is dependent upon the group rather than men may no longer tolerate unappealing masculine behavior merely to have a male companion. The relationship between members of a consciousness-raising group can help reduce a painful dependency.

> One woman described how she used to feel jealous and stage scenes when her lover, for whom she had divorced her husband, went out with business companions without inviting her. She reported that their

relationship had improved when, with the advice and support of her group, she had stopped demanding that her lover spend every evening with her.

Reduction of dependency can help a relationship; or it can harm it, if the relationship was constructed around the female's dependency. But the substitution of a consciousness-raising group for a marital relationship in validating reality has additional consequences. A frequently voiced goal of consciousness raising is "understanding what it is to be a woman in a patriarchal society that oppresses women," and among the patriarchal institutions that are perceived as oppressing women are marriage and the nuclear family.[11] When a woman learns to define difficulties in a relationship as political oppression, possibly defining the relationship itself as an oppressive institution, a heavy burden is placed on that relationship, especially when its world-building functions have been taken over by a new group of significant others. Feminist publications frequently print letters from readers telling how they found the courage to break free from an unhappy marriage with the advice and support of their consciousness-raising group. Newton and Walton's informants report "a great many more broken marriages, separations, changed heterosexual relationships" among the women in their consciousness-raising groups: in one group of eight women, four ended their marriages during the duration of the group; in another group of twelve, half ended "bad" relationships with men; and by the time another Older Women's Liberation group of twelve members dissolved, all but two members were divorced.[12]

Not only do relationships break up (and informants report that marriage breakups in some circles have reached epidemic proportions), but feminists also report difficulties in forming new relationships with men.

In the spring of 1972 an article appeared in the *Village Voice* describing the author and her friends, all in their late twenties, active in or sympathetic to women's liberation:

In the past six months . . . the thing we've held most in common is a kind of emotional atomization. The one marriage in the group broke up last spring, the couples who were living together went on separate trips abroad, got separate apartments, and generally subjected themselves and everyone else to an agony of indecision. . . .

I thought for a while that it might be only us, that these things were contagious among close friends. But then I looked around and it seemed to be everywhere. I'm hard pressed to come up with a single friend who loves anyone, who is loved, who remembers what the word means. Sex, yes. Lots of sex, more than ever; one of the advantages of being unattached is that you can sleep around more easily. . . .

The fact remains: men are a necessity to heterosexual women. One sees, however, some peculiar accommodations to that heterosexuality now, primarily the stillborn attempts by women to forge those new, freer relationships with men. The old nightmarish dependence begins to go out of the window, as one divests oneself of the idea of marriage-happily-after. But what is taking its place? Partly, it seems, a game of imitate-the-oppressor. . . .

A friend of mine reported the other day that the women he meets are becoming alarming. He describes a typical evening: he's asked his agent's assistant out for a drink. Afterwards, they stop at her apartment. He kisses her once or twice ("It seemed expected of me," he said); she immediately begins to take off her clothes. Feeling like a fool, he blurts, "Wait a minute, I don't even know you." "That's all right," she replies. "I prefer to fuck men I don't know. It's better that way." [13]

This dilemma—where established relationships with men have ended, partially because of female demands for self-actualization, but new relationships are purely sexual, with little feeling—seemed to strike a responsive chord with at least ten informants the week the article appeared. Several women said, in effect: "That's me, that's what's happening to me and to all my friends."

Many informants report that they will not enter a sexist or oppressive relationship, but that they are having difficulty forming any other kind. Women in consciousness-raising groups, in conferences, in personal conversation, mention the difficulty of initiating relationships with men. They complain of

> the flaccidity, the one-dimensionality, the lack of imagination, the lack of life in most of the men I saw about me. Where was their energy, their activity, their spontaneity? Where was their passion? [14]

A male psychiatrist says of today's young men:

> ... as men explore the receptive aspect of their nature, they also become more exploitative, more inclined to take, without giving much back except their charm. They become toward their girlfriends as Victorian women once were toward "responsible" men: exploiting, manipulative, demanding and "cute." [15]

This theme, of vital women and ineffectual men, is widespread in women's movement circles:

> The women I knew were filled with passion, not only sexual passion, although that too, but the passion for seizing life and shaping it, infusing it with the breath of an expansive humanity, and intelligent vitality. And they were gagging from the effort of repressing their desire for a truly human form of love.
>
> What are we freeing ourselves *for*, I thought, if not to become happier people? What use is it to liberate

one's potential if there is no one capable of valuing or matching or responding to that potential? [16]

Some commentators suggest a causal relationship between feminine independence and masculine weakness, as though men can be strong only when propped up by dependent women. Impotence, much discussed in the early 1970s, was blamed by one physician on the women's movement, with its attempt to dominate men; while a psychiatrist stated that women's demands were breeding "a society of weak, neurotic and scared men ... shallow, beaten males turning up at my office in ever-increasing numbers." [17] It is impossible to measure whether men are indeed weaker and less potent today than they were in the past. But one finds a growing *belief* that young men are becoming weaker, whether this stems from psychiatrists, who attribute the weakness to the women's movement and to "early unisex," [18] or feminists, who point out that men pay a high emotional price for attempting to live up to inflated standards of "masculinity" and that they must have the support of dependent women in order to fulfill the cultural ideal of masculine power and potency.

In addition, one might conjecture that the feminist disillusion with "weak" men contains elements of a self-fulfilling prophecy. When a woman in the first flush of feminism discovers she has been "oppressed," "programmed" to defer to men, to mute her own ideas and feelings, to base her life upon the comfort and ambitions of a man—she may react with anger and a sharp insistence on her rights. Such a woman may appear aggressive and demanding to an outsider, and only comparatively passive men may tolerate her demands. (Thus, not all men are willing to be used as a sex object, as did the agent's assistant who preferred sex with men she did not know.) Compliant men are undoubtedly available, as they doubtless always have been, but it is possible that the women who demand this role reversal are precisely those who are dissatisfied with the type of man who meets their demands. Thus, certain feminist demands upon men may effectively divide men into "sexists" and "doormats." The sexists are intolerable; the doormats, tedious. The dissatisfied feminist may conclude that men just cannot relate to liberated women.

> A 33-year-old divorced informant, after the last of a series of what she described as painful and destructive affairs, said she didn't see herself as having children, or even an intense relationship with a man, that these things just haven't worked out for her. She said she planned to have intimate relationships only with women; men would be light and passing things in her life. When asked whether the same problems might not exist in relationships with women if one concentrated exclusively on them, she replied that she did not think this would occur because she felt intimate with many women, while she became involved with one man at a time.

This disappointment with men and with the possibilities of having satisfactory relationships with them is so widespread that there is much discussion, at feminist meetings, consciousness-raising groups, and conferences, of what is called "alternate life styles." One solution proposed is multiple heterosexual relationships, to allow greater emotional control and autonomy. Thus, one feminist, discussing monogamy, concluded that "woman's acceptance of man's right to a commitment on such a day-to-day issue as sexual behavior is tantamount to her acceptance of his total control over her." [19] Feminism, by encouraging experimentation and suggesting more independent sexual alternatives, is seen in this view as encouraging a greater independence in other areas as well. In addition to multiple relationships, some feminists consciously seek sexual role reversal, with the man used only as sex object.[20]

Some feminists manage to alter heterosexual relationships in a more egalitarian direction. Thus, Sarah Miller, who felt trapped in a tenement with two young children while her husband was having an affair with another woman, reported that her marriage improved when her husband's feminist co-workers at a radical journal criticized him for his attitudes toward women (see Appendix on p. 188). They challenged him on

> ... both the way he treated women in his work situations and also the way that he dealt with his children.... They said that if he didn't take care of his own children part of the time he was going to have to take care of the other newspaper children.

Sarah's husband chose to help care for his own children, and her situation changed for the better. This confrontation occurred in the spring of 1970, but although she felt her situation improved, Sarah and her husband began to think that the nuclear family situation, itself, was in need of alteration.

> "There were dissatisfactions in living as we did," she said. "Increasingly it seemed to me that my independence depended on my husband's dependence ... that he was very responsible toward the children, took care of them a lot, but the more he did that, the more we functioned as a nuclear family. The more he got into the kids, it became this *thing*, and I would be waiting for him to get back in order to get to my meeting...

In 1971 Sarah and her husband began to discuss forming a commune, and in December 1972 they moved into a large brownstone with two other families: six adults and five children in all. The women had previously worked together in feminist groups. Every individual, adult and child, had a separate room, with adults sharing child care, house cleaning, food shopping and preparation, and house renovation on a rotating basis. In April 1976 Sarah seemed pleased with her living situation and reported that a number of women she had worked with in feminist groups had moved into similar communal situations.

It is not known how many feminists live in this sort of "limited" commune where household tasks, rather than marriages, are shared. Broken marriages are probably still more frequent than such solutions. (Sarah, herself, spoke with some surprise about a feminist health group in Boston in which most of the women were still married to the men they started with Before Feminism.) Although such communal solutions may be comparatively rare at this time, they do offer a way to reconcile an individual love relationship that includes both children and a measure of autonomy and self-fulfillment for men and women.

Another proposed alternative to unsatisfying relationships is a kind of "polymorphous perverse" sexuality, in which the sex of participants is relatively unimportant and genital sexuality is deemphasized in favor of warmth and cuddling.[21]

There is much serious discussion of masturbation in the movement, as an alternative to using men merely for sexual satisfaction.[22] Some of this is based on an influential article, "The Myth of the Vaginal Orgasm," which argues that once women discover the clitoris rather than the vagina as the source of the orgasm, men become sexually expendable and women are able to satisfy themselves or each other.[23] On the other hand, some feminist groups advocate celibacy, involving complete separation from men, with emotional but not physical relationships with women.

When feminists discuss masturbation and celibacy, an observer may be tempted to laugh at the rhetoric and subject matter. Laughter defends against perception of pain, the pain of women unable to establish or accept culturally approved relationships. As informant after informant is heard describing relationships that have soured and died, however, relating incidents involving sexual and emotional exploitation, and expressing grief and bewilderment, the observer may interpret discussions of masturbation and celibacy as attempts by women who feel bruised and unfree to seek emotional and physical autonomy. A book by a feminist in her twenties is entitled *Combat in the Erogenous Zone,* and indeed the war between the sexes in New York City in the early 1970s frequently seemed to have reached a terminal and insoluble stalemate.[24] Firestone writes of the destructive choice offered women today: they can marry, be placed on a pedestal, transformed into a possession or appendage, or become "the other woman" used and misused to prove a man's virility. To escape this "poisoned love," the author outlines several alternatives: a woman can play traditional female games to pay men back; she can join the Search for the Mirage—a nonsexist male; she can have sex without emotion; she can learn to masturbate without guilt; or she can attempt to form lesbian relationships.[25] I have heard women in movement circles seriously considering each of these alternatives. Some appeared to have found satisfactory, if temporary, solutions; others were still searching. Many indicated that they had tried several alternatives in succession.

And many seem to have ended with the last, and possibly most radical, choice: lesbianism.

5   Becoming a Lesbian

In 1972, at a lesbian-feminist conference, a lesbian newspaper columnist drew sustained laughter when she said: "Look around you—do you see any lesbians becoming straight?" The laughter was a recognition that the progression from heterosexual to homosexual seemed to occur frequently among women who had become active in the women's liberation branch of the movement, while the opposite progression was not in evidence.

Naturally, many women who are already lesbians become feminists. But in addition, a large number of women become lesbians after they become feminists.[1] It is difficult to measure their number, just as it is often difficult to distinguish lesbians unless they identify themselves. Abbott and Love quote an estimate on the number of lesbians in the movement from the March 1972 issue of *Psychology Today*; based on a survey of 15,000 women, with a large number of feminist respondents, the magazine estimated that up to 20 percent of the women in some feminist groups were lesbians.[2]

One of the problems in measuring who is and is not a lesbian is what criteria to use. A lesbian activist, discussing "coming out," the public announcement of homosexuality, said:

> There are all kinds of coming out: emotional, physical, intellectual, and political. Each one is different, and can occur at different times in a woman's development. Some women who call themselves lesbians and think of themselves as lesbians have never had a physical relationship with another woman—they've been too brainwashed by society and they're not yet ready for that.

Is a lesbian a woman who has felt strong emotional ties to another woman; one who has had emotional and perhaps sexual feelings for a woman; a woman who has had a sexual experience with a woman; one who has sex with men and women; a woman who loves only women?

Ti-Grace Atkinson has defined lesbians as "women who live a total commitment to women, even though they have never had sexual relations with women." [3] Such a definition would include a large number of dedicated feminists who, whatever their sexual activity, have gradually ceased forming emotional relationships with men. Thus, a description of a New York Radical Feminist meeting, on the subject of Male Friends, reported:

> The most repeated phrase of the whole evening was "Before Feminism." Several of us realized it was no longer possible to have male friends: they are the oppressor; they hurt us, exploit us, and no matter how "liberated," liberal or in accord with feminism they claim to be, they have no common experiences, so cannot treat us as equals.

The author states that five of eighteen women at the meeting said at first they had no male friends, but that once a clear definition of friendship was arrived at (the definition is not offered):

> ... the final hand-count showed a further ten to twelve women had had their consciousness raised sufficiently to realize that having male friends was a contradiction to the politics of Radical Feminism.[4]

This author clearly associates a raised consciousness with an exclusion of men, an association that has been frequently observed among women's liberation participants. However, separatism was not observed in women's rights circles and, in fact, NOW has always welcomed men.

This segregation is perhaps not very different from the situation among members of other revolutionary social movements; committed participants tend gradually to restrict significant interaction to other members, who help reinforce the new and revolutionary view of reality. The difference, in this case, is that *all women's liberation participants are female.* Thus when the women's liberationist associates as much as possible with "sisters," these significant others are female.

We have, then, a feminist spending much, possibly most, of her time with other women and deeply committed to women emotionally and ideologically. How does she take the next step, if indeed she does so, and get involved sexually with women?

I can present antecedent conditions for a woman becoming a lesbian after becoming a feminist. But the question will naturally arise: is that the *real* reason? Psychological motivation is a murky area, especially when dealing with a controversial subject such as homosexuality. Is an informant telling the truth? Does she know the truth? It is easy, and tempting, when dealing with such a subject to quote those selections from psychologists and psychiatrists that reinforce whatever one's contention happens to be. In the literature, however, we find that similar observations have been made by psychiatric authorities and by feminists, despite the fact that each group interprets these phenomena differently. For example, classic Freudian psychiatrists state that feminine women are characterized by narcissism, passivity, and masochism—or penis envy.[5] These psychiatrists believe that these traits have biological bases and represent "normal," "healthy," "adaptive" behavior. Other psychiatrists have observed the same characteristics but attribute them to cultural conditioning.[6] Feminists, too, have observed that traditional female behavior is characterized by narcissism, masochism, and passivity; they, however, interpret such behavior as culturally conditioned and self-destructive.

A female attempt to alter these feminine characteristics, to seek autonomy and independence, and define the self by activity rather than relationships has also been observed. This has been called "a masculinity complex" by those who believe such behavior is neurotic and maladaptive,[7] and "feminism" by those who believe the attempt to escape these cultural constraints represents healthy behavior. Thus, one psychoanalyst observed that "much of what is called femininity is actually a trait characteristic of a dependent personality, and to the extent that this dependency becomes neurotic it causes much of the difficulty suffered by women in our culture." [8]

In addition, some association between the attempt to escape traditional female traits, or role requirements, and lesbianism has been observed. Freudian psychiatrists tend to associate the masculinity complex with homosexuality, seeing both as attempts to escape women's "normal" biological role. Feminists, on the other hand, tend to interpret the same observation—of an association between feminism and lesbianism—in terms of escaping masculine dominance and sex-role stereotyping.

There is, then, some agreement in the observations of masochism, narcissism, and passivity that characterize traditional "feminine" behavior,[9] and on the association between an attempt to alter or escape these role requirements and female homosexuality. Rather than choosing between alternative interpretations of these observed phenomena, I am going to examine some antecedent conditions of a feminist becoming a lesbian.

One antecedent condition is differential accessibility. Women who no longer associate with men, because of political conviction and/or increasing difficulty in maintaining heterosexual relationships, have only one group left to relate to—women.

> One woman told how, when she became a feminist after her divorce, she found it harder and harder to have relationships with men. There just weren't enough acceptable men—who could relate to a feminist—or available men—who found her attractive—to go around. She was celibate for two or three years and never thought she would have another intimate relationship. When, in a consciousness-raising group, she met and fell in love with another woman, she was delighted to find there was another possibility. You're more equal in a lesbian relationship, she said. And you have more people to pick from.

Now, differential access to members as opposed to nonmembers occurs in many social movements in which segregation from the outside world is gradually intensified and, in fact, is necessary to guard commitment.[10] In heterosexual social movements, however, such segregation does not necessarily transform the sex or family life of co-participants, who are free to have affairs with and even marry one another.

In addition, there is an ideological antecedent condition: a belief that sexual preference is, like other stereotyped "masculine" and "feminine" behaviors, a result of early conditioning that can (and possibly should) be reversed when such conditioning is shed. A number of feminists have been heard discussing heterosexual relationships, including marriage, in this light.

> One woman in a consciousness-raising group said she preferred to have women friends, although she still

wanted one important man in her life—just one. She finds women more interesting, partially because there is "less hassle" involved in friendship with women. She thought her need or desire for a man must be due to the conditioning she received, but this conditioning is very strong, and she finds it difficult to think about a woman sexually. She knows, however, that it would be better, or more "politically correct," if she got it all together with a woman. The other members assented, appearing to agree that it was almost a personal defect—or one of conditioning—that made them feel sexually attracted to men.

Often joined to the conviction that heterosexuality is solely a result of early conditioning is a belief (or hope) that loving women might be simpler and less painful than loving men. There is an emphasis in feminist circles upon the naturalness, ease, kindness, and trust that women are able to give to one another.

> At least we cared enough about each other that we were able to talk about the things that went wrong, the peculiar twists and turns of feeling, the fears, the hesitations, the doubts, the moments of self-re-crimination, the moments of passion. We understood each other's bodies because they were our own bodies. . . . We were able to trust each other, sure in the knowledge that it was not a matter of conquest.[11]

A number of feminists have been observed becoming sexually involved with other women for what appear to be purely ideological reasons. Such behavior is "politically correct," therefore desirable, and consequently undertaken. Abbott and Love discuss "the political Lesbian who comes to Lesbianism through theory." [12]

> At the beginning of 1974, one woman described the reactions of her son, in his early 20s, who attended a poetry reading where he met a number of young

women who were in his Bennington graduating class. "Gill said these women used to be his friends," she reported, "and there they were, sitting with each other, hugging and kissing publicly. And they wouldn't say a word to him. I know some of them," said the (feminist) informant, "and I'm sure they're not *real* lesbians." By this, she meant that she believed their behavior stemmed more from political conviction than from an irresistible sexual urge.

I was told in lesbian circles that this type of lesbian, or "gay" woman, may be somewhat mockingly described as "head gay," to differentiate her from someone whose sexual inclinations classify her as "bed gay." For the first group, the initial impetus is intellectual. A lesbian who was active in the early days of feminism told how many women she met at that time made passes at her. "They wanted their lesbian experience," she reported. "It was a fad, the thing to do." At times she felt annoyed; she didn't like being a "token lesbian."

Another informant reported how, after her marriage broke up, she went from man to man thinking if she just found the right man her troubles would be over. She then became interested in philosophy and read omnivorously until she discovered Marx; this was what she had been looking for, and she stopped reading and joined a Marxist group. She was seriously considering becoming a "full-time professional revolutionary," when one evening, after a group meeting, several members repaired to a nearby bar; she was discussing the revolution to come when she looked around and realized that all the men were thinking about just one thing—who was going to go home with her that night. She left the bar, went home, and said to herself: "I'm going to become a feminist, and I'm going to become a lesbian." And she did.

Differential accessibility of women over men, a belief that heterosexuality results solely from conditioning, a hope that relationships with women might be less painful than those with men, and a conviction that it is "politically correct" to express one's growing commitment to women physically as well as emotionally may be necessary conditions for a feminist becoming a lesbian. But one cannot judge whether they are sufficient conditions. Although many feminists become lesbians, not all do so. This could be construed as evidence that other deep psychological processes are operating. Such processes will not be investigated. Instead, I am going to explore a functional explanation of lesbianism among feminists and ask: what are the consequences of a feminist becoming a lesbian?

Gerlach and Hine, in their study of contemporary social movements, examine the commitment process as a type of conversion.[13] The authors divide commitment into a subjective experience and an overt act. They believe a participant can undergo the experience, which is profound and identity altering, without undertaking the overt act. Nevertheless, the act serves to separate the converted from their former lives and associates. I believe that the subjective identity-altering experience in the women's movement is consciousness raising. This experience has been observed among reformist women's rights feminists and radical women's liberationists. The overt act that separates the convert from nonbelievers, however, has been observed primarily among women's liberationists. Gerlach and Hine call this a "bridge-burning act," noting that it marks a sharp break with the past, "cutting off from the old and strengthening ties with the new." Unlike the behavior expected in, and commonly produced for, rites of passage, the bridge-burning act of commitment to a movement does not follow social expectations; instead, it publicly violates social norms "and takes the individual out of the larger society in some significant way." [14]

Becoming a lesbian serves as a bridge-burning act for a feminist. "Coming out" as a lesbian may involve the loss of husband and children, of parents, job, and "straight" friends. The newly lesbian feminist is effectively separated from her past experience, relegated by herself and the outside world to a social category composed of others like her.

Lesbian theorists frequently present the lesbian as the ultimate feminist, the model for all others.[15] The lesbian is seen as the embodiment of complete freedom from male domination; she has achieved the autonomy and self-actualization that heterosexual women are still seeking.

> The lesbian, through her ability to obtain love and sexual satisfaction from other women, is freed of dependence on men for love, sex, and money. She does not have to do menial chores for them (at least at home), nor cater to their egos, nor submit to hasty and inept sexual encounters. She is freed from fear of unwanted pregnancy and the pains of childbirth, and from the drudgery of child raising.[16]

Heterosexual feminists appear defensive on occasion, as though they must apologize for consorting with the oppressor, for not following feminism to its farthest, and according to lesbians, its most logical end. They accuse lesbians of proselytizing, of attempting to impose their views and sexual preferences on all feminists.[17] If becoming a lesbian is conceptualized as a feminist bridge-burning act, perhaps there is some justification for these charges.[18] In this respect, lesbianism is indeed the ultimate step, because feminists who have become lesbians have not only undergone the subjective identity-altering *experience*, they have also, by publicly assuming the role of lesbian, undertaken an *act* that represents and embodies an alienation from traditional society because of their commitment. They are, in this view, outcasts *because* they are feminists, with their lesbianism representing a distillate of feminist principles.

In point of fact, lesbians are treated with sympathy and identification by many feminists, women's liberationists in particular—an attitude that can mystify reform feminists who do not see lesbianism as feminism carried to its most logical step. Lesbians have no emotional commitment to men; they have taken the zero-sum game of commitment-to-men vs. commitment-to-women as far as it can go. Female bonding is the lesbian's only reality; she loves, understands, and needs women. Not only is she willing, she is almost forced to work with women to build a "women's world." [19]

The feminist as lesbian, then, has placed herself in a position where she is cut off from the "straight" world. Her new and transformed reality is supported and reinforced by "an intense concentration of all significant interaction within the group." [20] If one associates the extent of a raised consciousness with the degree of a woman's segregation from the outside world, then the lesbian feminist, like the celibate feminist, has a very high consciousness indeed.

6

How to Tell the Women from the Girls: Feminist Demeanor and Sexual Deference

Chapters 1-5 have examined the process of becoming a feminist—or joining a group composed of women. Although interpersonal relationships may be changing during this process, it may be difficult for outsiders to observe these alterations. Certain behavioral changes, however, are more easily observable; and these parallel changes in self-image and in relationships with others.

DEMEANOR

First, I am going to examine changes in *demeanor*—"that element of the individual's ceremonial behavior typically conveyed through deportment, dress and bearing." [1]

During my fieldwork, from 1971 to 1973, I observed a characteristic demeanor among women's liberation participants; with some experience, this behavior was easily recognized. The most extreme manifestations were found among lesbian feminists. From the lesbians through radical to reform feminists, demeanor could be arranged on a continuum—the more radical the ideology, the more recognizable the demeanor.

Lesbian feminists generally wore jeans or denim workmen's overalls, the baggy kind that hid the shape of the wearer. The pants might be topped by a man's T-shirt or workshirt. It was apparent they were not wearing bras. Their hair was not so much styled as *there;* they wore no cosmetics; steel-rimmed glasses or sunglasses were frequent; footgear was comfortable, with a predominance of heavy men's workboots or sneakers; and jewelry was rare, with the exception of political buttons or women's liberation pendants. Associated with this costume was a recognizable deportment and bearing—a freedom of stride, of stance, of language. These women talked back to street hecklers; carried heavy loads with pride; changed their own tires; repaired and operated their own public address systems. Such demeanor was not exclusively lesbian feminist, but a woman who looked and behaved in this way was a revolutionary feminist and might well be a lesbian.

To keep the record straight, I must repeat an earlier point here: not all feminists are lesbian, and not all lesbians are feminists. But in the 1971-73 period under study, a particular demeanor among self-avowed lesbian feminists could be observed, which might be considered the most extreme version of feminist demeanor. It was, in fact, difficult to distinguish lesbian feminists from "straight" women's liberationists. Stereotypes frequently failed; soft-voiced, gentle-looking feminists identified themselves to me as lesbians. Language provided some clues. The lesbian feminists used profanity of a kind rarely heard in the conventional middle-class world—the Anglo-Saxon words for defecation and intercourse were employed so frequently that they seemed to have lost all meaning and have turned into a sort of verbal music. Although heterosexual feminists also used these terms, they seemed more likely to save such profanity to emphasize a point—or to represent defecation and intercourse.

Goffman has noted the "self-imposed uniform worn by members of erupting social movements" and the alienation from the ordinary course of social life that such dress expresses.[2] The clothing worn by radical feminists cannot be considered a uniform in the same way, for example, as the outfits of early European fascist groups (cited by Goffman in this connection). But the term "uniform" has been used in another way by fashion writers, referring to an archetypical costume of a particular social group. The little black Chanel dress worn by upper-class women before World War II and the Brooks Brothers suit of the organization man come to mind. Not all members of the group wear the "uniform," but the costume can be used to identify members. For members it is a socially safe, appropriate dress for most occasions.

In this sense there was a women's liberation "uniform"—an appropriate costume for almost every women's liberation occasion. There were always other women dressed that way; in fact, the majority of participants were generally wearing some elements of this outfit. In linguistic terms it was the *unmarked category*.[3]

There were variations in this costume. The prototypical outfit seen on lesbians and other utopian (and alienated) feminists could take on a more intentional, becoming look. The jeans might fit well instead of being baggy or ragged; the shirt might match or contrast. There was an expensive, fashionable version of the uniform.

> A lawyer in her twenties boasted that she wore jeans to her prestigious foundation job. She said that jeans could become quite a production, however: "You need the right jacket, and gloves, and a shirt that goes with jeans, and by the time you've finished at Bloomingdale's, I sometimes wonder if you've saved any time or money at all."

Theoretically, jeans were worn by women's liberation participants because they were comfortable, inexpensive, and could be acquired without extensive involvement in the consumer economy. The lawyer quoted above, however, reported that she had so much trouble with fit that her husband had inquired about custom-made jeans at the expensive sporting goods store Abercrombie and Fitch. They decided that the price, $75, was too high.

With the modified uniform, I found modifications in deportment and bearing, related to Goffman's distinction between a "loose" vs. "tight" orientation.[4] The more traditional the clothing, the more conventionally "feminine" the deportment and bearing.

The uniform was omnipresent at New York City women's liberation functions during my fieldwork. It was rarely observed, however, at meetings of the largest women's rights group, the National Organization for Women. NOW members wore cosmetics, attractively styled hair, stockings, and high-heeled shoes. Outfits ranged from unobtrusive pants and tops, through dresses and long skirts, to a conspicuous and seductive style of dress associated with vacation resorts for "singles." This involved an elaborate hairdo dyed blonde, red, or black, lavishly applied cosmetics, false eyelashes, much jewelry, and skin-tight knit pants with a tight knit shirt, emphasizing a cantilevered bra (very different from the low-slung bounding look popular among radical feminists). I never observed this seductive "resort look" among women's liberation participants.

Demeanor is symbolic and communicative; and the information communicated is frequently nonverbal. In common with other forms of nonverbal communication, demeanor has a number of interesting characteristics: (1) the sender may not be entirely aware of the content of the message; (2) the recipient, too, may not be aware of messages transmitted; (3) because nonverbal communication can be under imperfect control of the sender, it may be more difficult to falsify than verbal communication; and (4) translation of nonverbal messages into words may make them appear more intentional than they were actually meant to be.[5]

Demeanor can communicate status, group membership, occupation, personality, and sexual availability. It can express what a person thinks, fears, and hopes about himself or herself. Psychiatrists who analyze the meanings of such behavior tend to imply that they are the same for the group as for the individual.[6] Thus a group may be diagnosed as suffering from feelings of inferiority, penis envy, and so forth. Psychiatric insights about individuals need not be rejected in order to examine the *social meanings* of demeanor. For a sociological analysis of demeanor, I shall use the concept of *role*. Role mediates between "society" and "the individual," operating at the interface between individual behavior and social conduct.[7] A role expresses an actor's patterned relation to a group. Deportment, dress, and bearing are a way of packaging the self in relation to a particular group. The group then reacts to the integration of the role presentation and to its harmony with group aims.

The relation between demeanor and role involves practical and symbolic elements. Clothing promotes certain types of behavior and at the same time symbolizes the role associated with that behavior.

Thus, upper-middle-class women in the nineteenth century were not only seen as fragile, their clothing enforced fragility. Layers of petticoats, narrow shoes, and tightly laced corsets made it difficult for a "lady" to walk freely or work outside the home for an extended period of time. The elaborate and restrictive dress of the nineteenth-century lady made a symbolic statement about the wearer's delicacy (symbolized by a tiny waist and exhibited by frequent shortness of breath and fainting), her fineness and fragility (shown by ideally small hands and feet crammed into tiny boots), and her value as an object. The clothing encouraged certain behavior; it also symbolized the role associated with that behavior. When Susan B. Anthony and Elizabeth Cady Stanton adopted the loose, comfortable bloomer outfit, they were met with ridicule so powerful and sustained that they gave up the costume, fearing to endanger the women's movement of the 1850s. The ferocity of the ridicule was an appropriate response, not to any intrinsic foolishness of the costume—fashion has never been noted for its common sense—but to the attempt of those nineteenth-century feminists to escape the restrictive role requirements of an upper-middle-class lady. Ridicule served as social control: the role of lady was safeguarded by making it difficult for an incumbent to wear a costume associated with alternate modes of behavior.

Today's women's liberationists, rebelling against the constraints of female role requirements, have rejected the deportment, dress, and bearing associated with the role of middle-class female. As in the past, reaction against the demeanor of the rebels functioned as social control. The media myth of bra burning exemplifies this ridicule. Feminists unanimously asserted that bras were burned only as a joke, years after the media incorrectly reported the story.[8]

The demeanor of the women's liberationists can be understood only in relation to conventional female deportment, dress, and bearing. Women's liberation demeanor inverts conventional expectations. Consequently, we cannot understand it without examining traditional female demeanor.

Before investigating conventional expectations, let us note that in our complex, heterogenous society, a person may choose from a repertoire of demeanors, representing various roles; in a homogeneous society, roles are frequently additive, allowing a person to use a relatively limited set of behaviors for a traditional role cluster.[9] As a result, a homogeneous society offers less possibility for behaving inappropriately. In our society, on the other hand, actors assume multiple and conflicting roles; people belong to different groups and have different ranks within these groups.[10] A presentation that fits one situation may be inappropriate for another. The actor must decide which role to produce for a specific occasion. And he or she may make the wrong decision.

Because demeanor communicates nonverbally, an error in role choice and production is often perceived as a violation of "taste" or "manners." This allows an audience to agree that an offense has been committed without having to examine the rules governing such behavior—rules that may work better when they are not verbalized. This may explain why certain errors of "taste" or "manners" provoke violent reactions—the message may not have been put into words, but the audience has reacted to what may be a serious social offense.

I do not believe that the feminist inversion of conventional middle-class female deportment, dress, and bearing is intentional; nor is it consciously so perceived by the women or their audience. What is perceived, and reacted to, is a rejection of traditional role requirements. Women's liberationists act "unfeminine." The extent of the threat posed by this unfeminine demeanor may not be recognized on an intellectual level, just as it is not entirely clear why certain behavior seems unfeminine. On a gut level, however, spectators sense a challenge to cherished assumptions about love, sexuality, power, and freedom—and the gut reaction may well be rage.

I have described a range of feminist demeanor and have correlated variations with ideology. Next to be examined are three attributes of middle-class deportment, dress, and bearing that may give us a better understanding of the women's liberation inversions of this behavior.

The first attribute is *attractiveness*. A woman who looks "pretty" has generally made a conscious attempt to appeal to the opposite sex—just as one who does not attract has often made an attempt not to appeal. In our society, looking attractive is usually related to a woman's doing something to herself, as opposed to doing nothing. Time, effort, and equipment are needed.

We frequently hear that women dress for other women. How does this relate to attractiveness?

> A group of women in a beginning consciousness-raising group admitted that they constantly check the attractiveness of other women, as though looking through the eyes of the competition. A few said they will point out an attractive woman to their escort, as though this might defuse the threat posed by a situation where women's attractiveness is traditionally used to compete for men.

Women's liberation ideology rejects what is described as a demeaning and time-consuming attempt to falsify female physical characteristics in order to appeal to men. Movement literature tells how women are taught to be ashamed of their "natural" selves: they learn to hide their faces behind cosmetics, their breasts behind padded or uplift bras; they diet and disguise their bodies in constraining dresses and uncomfortable footgear.[11] A common discovery in consciousness-raising groups is that every woman feels inadequate to the fashion-magazine ideal; each is convinced her breasts are too large or small, her body the wrong size or shape, her face unattractive except when camouflaged by cosmetics.

> One informant described how members of her consciousness-raising group all removed their tops for one meeting. There was reluctance and embarrassment, but finally they all discussed their bodies and their feelings about them and discovered that each member felt her breasts were deficient in one way or another. "But we saw that we all had just breasts," said the informant; "no one was wonderfully magnificent, but everyone was perfectly adequate."

The women's liberation uniform is seen, by those wearing it, as a rejection of disguises, a way of actually and figuratively "letting it all hang out." Many women who wear the uniform, however, want to attract men—and do so. Perhaps it is this "attractiveness" that differentiates the bearing and deportment of heterosexual women's liberationists from that of lesbian feminists. The costumes may be similar, but the aura is different. The heterosexual women look *pretty*. Although such "natural" young women may be less appealing to those unused to this style, men of similar age and status find these looks highly attractive.

The "natural look" has become fashionable, as have many elements of the women's liberation uniform. I believe the dissemination of women's liberation demeanor is associated with the spread of feminist ideas, although no causal priority is suggested.

I have discussed attractiveness in conventional female

demeanor in terms of appealing to men. There is a way in which middle-class women dress for other women, however, and that is related to my second attribute: *status definition*. Men react to the aura conveyed by status or economic markers, but women are traditionally able to read the price tag of a particular article or "look." Women say: "She was wearing sixty-dollar boots." "I saw that dress for two hundred dollars." "Her pearls are real."

Status markers communicate positional information nonverbally. They indicate command over the actions of others and command over resources and benefits; these two command criteria are linked to prestige, esteem, and deference.[12] Conventionally it is the middle-class woman who wears the status markers that indicate the position of her man. Status-marker-as-positional-indicator can reach the rarefied heights described by *Women's Wear Daily*, where specialized females are featured as "consumption stars," with carefully staged ceremonial appearances at luncheons, dinners, and charity balls. Such a *femme objet*, garbed in costly status markers, is herself a status marker, symbolizing and projecting the worldly success of her escort.

The women's liberation uniform is an antistatus-marker costume. In uniform it is difficult to distinguish a feminist on welfare from one with a comfortable income. Women's liberation ideology rejects economic and class divisions—women are to be united as women. A young teacher at a community college told me she did not like to wear status symbols because she felt they separated her from her students. Many young feminists do not seem to realize, however, that the absence of status symbols also transmits information. Such symbolism is age-graded—it is more common among those under thirty-five—and class-related. One might speculate that the lower-class students with whom the community college teacher expressed solidarity by wearing jeans were themselves adorned with as many status symbols as possible. Although it may be easier to reject status markers when one has status or comes from a family with it, women's liberation participants have made a genuine attempt to reject hierarchy and status, and this attempt is expressed in their dress.

The third attribute of conventional female demeanor we should examine is *appropriateness*. This is related to an unspoken agreement between participants as to the purpose and ceremonial importance of a social encounter. Appropriateness involves consensus—only a few people can be inappropriately dressed for an occasion; they have then disagreed with the majority definition of the situation. Appropriateness is the attribute most frequently discussed as "taste," thus placing its locus in the individual rather than the group.

In many circles males wear a relatively fixed costume for social occasions, with the situation primarily defined by female demeanor. Female consensus defines the occasion, and females note deviations, reporting them to one another and to male participants. A middle-class female must guess how a new social situation will be defined; she must contrive a costume (and, by extension, a role production) to cover a range of social possibilities; and she must be prepared to carry off mistakes. This is a heavy responsibility. It requires social expertise—a reading of the possibilities, and fashion expertise—a knowledge of how to produce particular role effects.

A female preparing for a social encounter emphasizes a particular role or role cluster. Some role definitions are inappropriate for an occasion; they emphasize rank or group membership that co-participants would prefer to ignore.

I have indicated that the choice of appropriate middle-class female demeanor involves risk and skill. Women's liberation participants have been heard expressing distaste for "those women you see on Madison Avenue wearing everything new, and it all matches." In consciousness-raising groups they have also been heard confessing to a lack of self-confidence in the choice of appropriate conventional clothes, in knowing what to buy and what to wear. The women's liberation uniform provides an appropriate costume for every feminist occasion. A woman can dress differently when and if she wishes, but she has a "safe" costume to fall back on. The costume, then, provides a kind of social security.

SEXUAL DEFERENCE

I have discussed three attributes of middle-class female demeanor and examined feminist reactions to, and inversions of, these attributes. In this section I describe a reciprocal transaction between the sexes, which I call *sexual deference*, and show how women's liberationists invert this transaction. *Deference* has been described as a symbolic way of conveying appreciation, with the recipient standing for a larger social group.[13] A reciprocal sexual deference can be observed in our society: the woman expresses appreciation of a man through helplessness, admiration, and self-denigration; the man, in return, embodies competence, admiration, and protectiveness. Sexual deference involves an exchange: services such as package-carrying, tire-changing, and repair of mechanical equipment are exchanged for typing, provision of food and beverages, and small sewing repairs. Underlying this is an implicit division of areas of competence into "masculine" and "feminine."

Women's liberation deportment, dress, and bearing represent an inversion of traditional female demeanor, with attributes of conventional behavior negated by the women's liberation uniform. With demeanor, symbolic *behavior* is inverted. Sexual deference is inverted by feminists in a different way. Rather than a change in symbolism, a familiar symbolic form has been assigned a contrary *meaning*. With demeanor the symbolism is inverted; with deference, the symbolism is the same with the meaning inverted. The meaning of sexual deference has been turned on its head, and women's liberationists perceive this symbolic transaction as a ritual of status degradation rather than elevation. The following is a quote from a feminist article:

> In less civilized ages and societies, if a woman got too uppity, she was beaten up ... or she was raped ...

now, men are usually more subtle. . . . Instead of it being necessary to beat her up to indicate his physical superiority, he finds he can make his point . . . by opening a door for her, thus subtly indicating his superior strength and, by implication, her weakness and physical dependency. . . . Instead of it being necessary for him to withhold food from her to indicate her economic dependency, he insists on buying her drinks. . . . A woman often . . . feels a helpless humiliation under the gallantries, at the very least a slight feeling of discomfort. . . . She feels put down, but knows she should be flattered. . . . This is another example of the evil psychology of male supremacy, where the woman is supposed to welcome, feel flattered by her own degradation. . . .[14]

Women's liberationists reject the idea of a *complementary* relationship between the sexes, with each group assigned different but mutually appropriate behavior. Instead, they seek a symmetrical relationship with each sex producing essentially similar behavior.[15] The traditional meaning of sexual deference as appreciation is inverted, as is the underlying complementary relationship between the sexes. The conventional male-female relationship is not seen as mutually interdependent, with the woman protected and "put on a pedestal" in return for complementary services. Instead, the relationship is perceived as one of oppressor and oppressed: the woman is not elevated; she is "put down."

Consequently, many traditional female tasks are rejected by women's liberation participants, who tend to prefer repairing mimeograph machines to typing stencils, moving furniture to sewing slipcovers, changing a faucet washer to scrubbing the sink. Such behavior may seem capricious, if not downright foolish, to observers who cannot understand that this represents an inversion of the traditional reciprocity of sexual deference through the assignment of contrary symbolic meanings.

A paradox occurs here, which perhaps should be mentioned. If sexual deference represents status degradation, then, theoretically, women in symmetrical relationships should be free to try all tasks that appeal: sewing *and* furniture moving, cooking *and* nuclear physics. There is, however, an unspoken assumption that if the division of labor has oppressed women, then traditionally male work must be more enjoyable and generally superior. Feminists who enjoy cooking and child care report they have been chided for this by militant "sisters."

Women's liberation literature predicts the end of "role playing." The term refers to a complementary relationship, with different behavior expected from each sex. Lesbian feminists also reject role playing, where one partner dresses and behaves as the masculine "butch," the other as "femme." [16] The term role playing can also refer to behavior associated with roles that are sympathetic or complementary to men, as opposed to those a woman may find most interesting or satisfying. *No More Fun and Games* is the title of a women's liberation journal; the fun and games to be eliminated include role playing and sexual deference. The costume for no-more-fun-and-games (for heterosexual and homosexual feminists) is, of course, the androgynous women's liberation uniform, where position, role, and sex differences are symbolically abolished.

I have indicated that members of the largest women's rights group, the National Organization for Women (NOW), were rarely observed wearing the women's liberation uniform. Unlike women's liberation groups, the ideology and organizational structure of NOW has made no attempt to do away with status and hierarchy; what NOW seeks is a *higher position* for women: more interpersonal command, more command over resources and benefits, and more direct command—as opposed to that mediated by a relationship with a man. NOW does not disapprove of hierarchy; instead, the organization wants to move women up the ladder. Thus, status markers as symbols of position may well be appropriate garb for many NOW members. In fact, I observed more role playing and sexual deference exhibited by some NOW members than by their nonfeminist counterparts. The seductive demeanor I observed at NOW meetings may represent a kind of exaggerated sexual deference.

> In a consciousness-raising group several students admitted that when they first became involved in the women's movement, each had been careful to dress in an extremely "feminine" fashion, and each had stepped-up dating to prove she was a "real woman." "It was kind of an aggressive assertion of a passive role," said one.

The superseductive "resort look" may represent a similar "aggressive assertion of a passive role." Indeed, NOW demeanor in general may convey the fact that NOW members are not so much challenging the hierarchical structure of society as asking for a piece of the action.

I have discussed the way in which demeanor transmits messages below the level of words. Such nonverbal transmission is evident in the relations between women's liberation participants and lower- and working-class men. Women's liberationists frequently mention how unpleasant it is to endure the glances, remarks, and behavior of men in the street. I have heard nonfeminists express surprise at the intensity of this reaction. Nonfeminists do not particularly mind remarks and whistles—some say they take them as compliments. I discovered, however, that men in the street react very differently to a woman wearing the women's liberation uniform. The whistles and calls have a cruel, frightening quality; the men move in uncomfortably close, and some threaten to pat or grab. This elicits fear and hostility, which is returned by more hostility from the men. The whistles and remarks directed to *the same woman* in middle-class dress are more good-natured and teasing, with no threat of actual touching or violence.

Why might these men behave differently toward radical feminists? The status markers worn by a middle-class woman—the fashionable clothing, jewelry, wedding and engagement rings—announce that she is attached, as wife, mistress, or daughter, to a man with economic and, possibly, political clout. A lower-class man who threatens such a woman may sense that he would be subject to reprisals. Women's liberation demeanor, on the other hand, indicates that a woman is on her own and is unlikely to have access to the power to get anyone into trouble if she is harassed. This demeanor may be threatening to the *amour propre* of lower-class males, indicating that the wearer is not willing to play even a fantasy game of sexual deference. In addition, women's liberation participants are often out late at night without men, returning from meetings. Since many cannot afford taxis, and meetings in New York City are frequently held in unsafe neighborhoods, the women are placed in positions where male harassment can be particularly frightening and dangerous (since an implied threat of rape is always present). Thus, although women's liberationists are extremely sensitive to behavior they consider derogatory, it is possible that street incidents are more menacing to them than to women "protected" by middle-class demeanor.

I said that the women's liberation costume is an anti-role-playing uniform. As such, it symbolizes a "deviancy role." [17] Similar costumes are worn by other groups that define themselves as deviant, such as hippies, radicals, and students. There is another side to the deviancy role, however. Women's liberation demeanor stands for *belonging*. The revolutionary utopian feminist is part of a closely knit group of like-minded women working together to change themselves and society. The feelings of belonging, of closeness, associated with participation in a revolutionary social movement and symbolized by an inversion of customary female behaviors, is reinforced by the hostility shown by the outside world.

The nonverbal feminist rejection of the traditional female role appears to be clearly perceived by lower- and working-class men, "establishment" men, and, often, by other women. When women's liberation participants are met by coldness, harassment, and, on occasion, outright repression, this is interpreted as another indication of the unmotivated hostility of the "straight" world, further reinforcing an ideological rejection of that world. The demeanor thus functions as a self-fulfilling prophecy, eliciting hostile measures that reinforce belief in the need to change a repressive male power structure.

Women's liberation demeanor, then, acts as a boundary-maintenance mechanism, signaling membership and exclusion.

> The identification of another person as a fellow member . . . implies a sharing of criteria for evaluation and judgment. It thus entails the assumption that the two are fundamentally "playing the same game.". . . On the other hand, a dichotomization of others as strangers, as members of another . . . group, implies the recognition of limitations on shared understandings, differences in criteria for judgment of value and performance. . . .[18]

When communication is nonverbal, as with deference and demeanor, an actor frequently "knows" when another belongs or does not belong to his or her group, without perceiving exactly how the information has been transmitted. An individual or group that represents a danger to a cherished status quo is "recognized"; they are "the enemy." A fellow revolutionary is identified in like manner. Thus, the women's liberation uniform, which expresses militancy and is associated with segregation from nonbelievers, acts as a boundary-maintenance mechanism and self-fulfilling prophecy, reinforcing the segregation.

This section has examined the process of becoming a feminist. This can be conceived of as a journey. The interior space is traversed by an alteration of identity, while exterior distance is measured by increasing separation from nonbelievers. We can then picture the terrain of the women's movement stretching from the status quo to the most "far out" transformative visions. The more moderate the feminist group, the less alteration in identity required, and the less segregation from the outside world. Pragmatic women's rights organizations such as NOW operate within the existing social system. Members do not seek to transform themselves or their world; they wish to improve their situation so that it will more closely resemble the situation of men perceived as peers. The more radical the feminist goals, the more the women seek to transform themselves and their world.

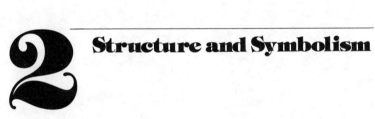

2 Structure and Symbolism

7

Women's Rights and Women's Liberation: Personal Change and Social Change

Part 1 showed how women are recruited to the women's movement and involved in feminist activities. These women change their images of themselves and their relationships to their worlds. The new feminist perceives herself as a member of a group composed of women, and as a member of this group, the activities of her personal life become political events.

The second half of the book focuses more directly on the movement, and on the groups of which it is composed. Conceptually, part 1 reflected a social-psychological approach, investigating the individual's relation to groups; part 2 reflects an approach in terms of social movements and social organization, examining the structure of the movement and the contribution of various groups to its functioning.

Women's movement groupings can be classified in a number of ways. For example, Gallagher arranged feminist groups in terms of means (from violent to gradualist) and ends (ranging from reform to revolutionary). The schematic representation of this system reveals, however, that means and ends are correlated: Gallagher's graph shows that the more gradualist the means, the more reformist the goals; the more violent the means advocated, the more revolutionary and utopian the goals.[1] This fourfold schema can, therefore, be collapsed into two principal classifications widely recognized within the women's movement, which have been called "reform" and "radical." Freeman points out, however, that these terms conceal basic differences in structure and style, and prefers to divide the groups into "older" and "younger," based on order of origin (and median age of activists):

> ... this diversity has sprung from only two origins whose numerous offshoots remain somewhat clustered around their sources. The first can be dated from the formation of the National Organization for Women (NOW) in 1966 by women associated with the President's Commission on the Status of Women and subsequent state commissions. The second came from the other side of the generation gap, from young women involved in the civil rights and youth movements of the last decade.[2]

Hole and Levine use the terms "women's rights" and "women's liberation" to characterize the two branches, and Carden follows this usage.[3] In a later description of the women's movement in 1975, Carden contends that the original distinction between women's liberation and women's rights is no longer valid, because many women's liberation groups have vanished, while women's rights organizations have adopted feminist analyses similar to those that originally characterized women's liberation groupings.[4] Later in the same publication, however, Carden discusses a conflict between "utopian" and "pragmatic" groups.[5] Interestingly, the program of the revolutionary utopians corresponds quite closely with the earlier women's liberationists, while the pragmatists resemble the women's rights adherents. Consequently, I believe the original distinction between the two branches is still valid, whether it is called "younger" and

"older," "utopian" and "pragmatist," or "women's liberation" and "women's rights." I use the terms "women's
liberation" and "women's rights" to describe these branches,
since this is the classification used by most observers and by a
large number of my informants during the fieldwork period.*

The terms "older" and "younger" suggest an age difference
between the members of each branch, and the data tend to
support this difference. (Gallagher and Carden offer the most
comprehensive data on membership in each branch.[6]) Wom-
en's rights members are somewhat older than their women's
liberation counterparts. They are more likely to be married,
well educated, be established in their life patterns (being
primarily professional women or housewives with older
children), have higher incomes (whether they or their husbands earn the money), and indicate more positive feelings
about men and somewhat less negative feelings about
marriage.

Women's liberation participants are younger. Their income is lower; many are students or hold low-paying clerical
jobs. They are less likely to be married or have children, and
more likely to be divorced or separated than their women's

---

* Let me point out, however, that the largest women's rights
organization, the National Organization for Women (NOW) used
the term "women's liberation" to describe NOW. I believe this was
less a classificatory device—NOW was not describing itself in relation
to other groups—than an attempt to indicate that NOW *was*
women's liberation, and that other feminist groups were nonexistent, or insignificant. During my fieldwork, NOW leaders were
observed behaving in a competitive fashion toward other feminist
groups. To give just two examples: in 1971, when women telephoned New York NOW for help or advice, the chapter president
referred these women only to NOW members, even when there were
other highly qualified feminists available. And at the 1973 national
NOW convention, a dramatic reading about the origins and history
of American feminism culminated with a list of prominent NOW
members, as though the history of feminism led directly and
exclusively to NOW.

rights counterparts. Many express extreme views on marriage and the family, child rearing, careers, and the need to overthrow the existing society.

Women's rights members, who are more likely to have professions or upper-middle-class husbands and families, have a stake in "the system." Women's liberation participants, on the other hand, tend to be women in transition—students, recent graduates, lesbians, women holding low-paying jobs while dreaming of highly paid prestigious professions, or divorcees seeking new identities and ways of life.

There is a difference in structure as well as personnel in the two branches of the movement. Women's rights groups are formally organized; group functions are arranged rationally on bureaucratic lines, and aims are specifically known.[7] The majority of women's rights groups are organized on a national basis, with elected officers, boards of directors, bylaws, membership rules, and criteria. Their goals are reformist; their means, legislative. Thus theirs is the organizational structure traditional in our society, so familiar that it tends to be taken for granted when one deals with an organization or social movement.

Women's liberation groupings, on the other hand, do not exhibit this traditional bureaucratic structure. Instead, they consist primarily of small groups of women integrated by a network of personal contacts. Women's liberation groupings do not have formal structure or leadership; many do not even have the concept of membership—any woman is welcome to join activities when and if she wishes. Women's liberation goals are revolutionary: both the individual and society are to be totally transformed.

The "structure" of women's liberation groups is less familiar than that of women's rights organizations, and consequently it is less apparent—to observers and partici-pants. Because the structure of such groups raises some interesting theoretical questions—especially when supported, as it is in women's liberation, by an ideology advocating structurelessness—one such group is examined in depth on pages 122–148 to explore the relationship between women's liberation ideology and its organization.

But, first, let us see in what other ways women's movement groupings can be classified. A second method of classification can be based on the type of change sought: individual or social. This division between groups seeking personal or social change crosscuts the previous distinction between women's rights and women's liberation. Although women's liberation groups originally concentrated primarily on consciousness raising, while women's rights groups focused on social change, this distinction has evaporated, and groups devoted to consciousness raising and "action" groups were later found in both branches of the movement.

Another way to classify women's movement groupings is by central organizing principle. Thus, subject matter defines a number of feminist groups; they are devoted to improving the status of women in a particular art or profession, or to a specific goal such as abortion reform or peace. Student groups are frequently affiliated with a specific high school, college, or university. Some groupings are female caucuses of larger professional or political organizations. There are mixed-sex groups (devoted to causes such as the Equal Rights Amendment) that are closely associated with feminist goals. Such groupings shift so rapidly, their central organizing principles are so varied and crosscutting, and problems of definition are so pervasive that it is difficult to sort them out. Because of these difficulties, some investigators have narrowed their focus and concentrated primarily on women's rights and women's liberation groupings. Although it is simpler and neater to ignore ambiguous feminist quasi-groups, many of which cannot be tidily classified as either women's liberation or women's rights, they must be included in a conceptual scheme in order to understand the true structure of the women's movement.

8

The Structure of the Women's Movement

Anthropologists and sociologists spend much time and effort classifying social movements, using terms such as *nativism, millenarianism, cargo cults, messianism, syncretism,* and *revitalization.*[1] Although Wallace criticizes existing classifications for generating an impossibly complex typology while leaving boundaries fuzzy, he then suggests another fixed typology.[2] Aberle's classification system is elegant and parsimonious, with a fourfold typology based on the amount of change sought—total or partial—and the kind of change—individual or social.[3]

Smelser divides social movements in a way that resembles Aberle's distinction between the search for partial or total change, contrasting social movements based on norm-oriented beliefs with those based on value-oriented beliefs.[4] A norm-oriented belief seeks to protect or restore existing social norms, with norm-oriented movements working through rules, laws, and regulatory agencies. Such movements are related to members' perception that they can influence the normative order. A value-oriented belief, on the other hand, attempts to modify conceptions about "nature, man's place in it, man's relation to man, and the desirable and non-desirable as they may relate to man-environment and inter-human relations," and calls for "a basic reconstitution of self and society."[5] Value-oriented movements are likely to occur when participants perceive no other means available for changing the social situation.

It is clear that Smelser's value-oriented category resembles Aberle's description of movements seeking total change; in fact, Aberle also associates such movements with lack of access to power. Smelser's norm-oriented movements correspond with those seeking partial change and are associated with members having some access to power.

According to these classifications, however—and to other fixed typologies—today's women's movement is hopelessly mixed. As indicated, the women's movement can be divided into value-oriented women's liberation groupings seeking total change and norm-oriented women's rights organizations working for partial change; consciousness-raising groups focus on individual change at the same time that action groups work for social change.

Rather than classifying social movements into ideal types, which exhibit imperfect correspondence with observed phenomena, Gerlach and Hine examine the *dynamics* of two contemporary social movements.[6] Their definition of a social movement includes efforts to achieve both individual and social change; and derived from their processual approach is a multigroup structural model that corresponds closely with the organizational structure of the women's movement. Unlike fixed typologies, which seem unable to deal with the diversity of means and ends, the multiple and sometimes conflicting goals, and the crosscutting principles of organization found in today's women's movement, the multigroup model organizes and illuminates the relationship between the various feminist groupings.

The multigroup model is based upon process. In fixed typologies time tends to be an intrusion that violates the symmetry and elegance of the pattern, whereas time is built into the multigroup scheme. It is perhaps not so much the *structure* as the structur*ing* of a social movement that is illuminated.

In this view, social movements are organized by three principles: decentralization, segmentation, and reticulation. (This contrasts with the model of leader and followers, prophet and disciples, employed by the majority of studies of social movements, where an organizational structure of a leader with a small band of disciples is implicit, leading to a pyramidal pattern, with new converts entering the bottom level, elevating the inner circle of individuals around the prophet or leader.) [7] Let us examine the feminist political field in relation to these three principles.

Decentralization. Social movements have many leaders associated with a large number of groupings rather than a single, central leader. The leaders frequently exhibit a nonhierarchical relationship with followers; a leader is "conceptually and emotionally equal with the humblest new convert." [8] Kinship terms such as "sister" express this lack of hierarchy. Evidence that leaders have limited power in the movement as a whole includes the following: leaders of various groups frequently disagree about means, goals, and ideological emphasis; no one leader knows all the groups that consider themselves part of the movement; a leader cannot make decisions that bind all movement participants or speak for the movement as a whole; and no leader has regulatory powers over the entire movement. In addition, there is no such thing as membership in the movement, only in individual groups. A participant cannot be invested by a leader: he or she is self-defined and may or may not be recognized by other participants.

Leaders in women's liberation groups have few regulatory powers over their own groups. A leader's decision-making power is based purely on personal magnetism and this can be compromised if she is publicly recognizable as a leader. The lack of institutionalized leadership in women's liberation increases the decentralization of the women's movement.

Unlike women's liberation groups, women's rights organizations encourage leadership, believing that female leadership is essential if women are to enter the masculine structure of power and control:

At the 1973 national NOW convention, Betty Friedan, a NOW founder, spoke to the assembled women telling them how she had been traveling around the country and "it's incredible—there are so many new leaders coming up. It seems as though two thousand new leaders a month are springing up for the women's movement!"

NOW has a traditional bureaucratic organizational structure, and NOW leaders have been heard uttering pronouncements about the women's movement, or women's liberation, as though NOW *was* the movement. Other groupings and leaders are ignored, not because they are not perceived but because decentralization is considered a defect, dissipating the force of the movement. Consequently, NOW leaders have acted on occasion as though the decentralization they deplored did not exist and the centralized structure of NOW was the women's movement. Nevertheless, despite the fact that NOW is the largest organization in the women's movement, with more than 60,000 members estimated in 1975, NOW leaders speak solely for NOW.[9]

Although movement groupings attempt to present a façade of unity to the outside world (with the exception of Friedan, who publicly and vociferously disavows radical and lesbian individuals, views, and groupings), no group can speak for another or for the movement, and no leader can influence behavior or decision making in other groups.

Decision making, then, is binding on a particular group, not on the movement as a whole. And within each grouping, those who disagree with a particular tactic, issue, or goal are free to hive off and start a new grouping. Because no centrally organized women's movement exists, there is no possible "movement policy" to be followed or violated, thus including or excluding groupings.

Such a situation can seem chaotic to those who believe the traditional hierarchical structural model is the only way a social movement can function and grow. The situation is, in fact, chaotic at times. Not only does the women's movement lack centralized mechanisms for regulation and decision making, it also has no centralized communication mechanism. No one individual, publication, or grouping has access to all the other groupings.

A decentralized structure is less efficient, leading to difficulties in communication and duplication of effort, but decentralization can also be a source of strength. Women's movement leaders and groupings tend to spring up as needed; one leader and grouping may be suitable for a particular task, attracting a specific type of participant, while another leader and grouping fill an entirely different niche. Groups are flexible. They are frequently convened to meet specific needs; when the need no longer exists, or a particular project is completed, the group may change goals or personnel—or disappear to be replaced by another group with new leaders and/or goals.

An interesting phenomenon related to leadership can be observed in the women's movement; this has been called "communication of charisma." [10] Women's movement participants do not obey a hypnotic and powerful leader. Instead, leaders inspire the women to be more autonomous, to take responsibility, to make decisions. Rather than regulating followers, leaders inspire them to regulate themselves— and to inspire new women. This inspiration is related to commitment. Participants are committed less to leaders than to an idea, and that idea specifically includes personal growth and autonomy. One way that growth is achieved is by helping others to achieve it. Thus, each committed individual is at least potentially able to "catch fire" with an intense and communicable commitment to movement ideas and goals that motivates her and others in working for the movement.

Segmentation. The women's movement is not only decentralized but also segmented—composed of a large number of "localized groups or cells which are essentially independent, but which can combine to form larger configurations or divide to form smaller units." [11]

Various explanations are offered for group fission. For example, one informant reported a guerrilla theater group split over hostility between lesbian and "straight" women.

Another believed that the real division was between those who wanted the group to be primarily a way of life and those who wanted a performing organization. "Personality differences" was advanced as the reason an antirape group split in two. Factionalism, based upon conflict between leaders, may be "ignored" because participants in women's liberation groups who disapprove of leadership may not wish to recognize the fact that leaders exist.

In both the theater and the antirape groups, informants reported a period of intense conflict, during which regular meetings were disrupted or postponed; at this time some women feared the group was dead. During such a period an observer would have difficulty finding out whether a group was dormant or dead. Operational criteria, such as number of weeks without a meeting, projects initiated or furthered, or number of participants, would be misleading—as would be reports from participants, who might conceal fears about the group's future. If the group revived, one could conclude it had been dormant; if two groups reconstituted, then the group had been in the process of dividing; if no group remained, then it had been dying. The processes looked the same; only the outcomes differed.

Fusion, as well as fission, can be observed in the women's movement. Groups combine for semipermanent coalitions, special projects, and ritual activities.

The Feminist Community, a proposed coalition of women's groups in New York City, was first discussed in March 1973, when a NOW member, who also belonged to more radical women's liberation groups, arranged a panel to discuss the subject. Eight groups were represented. In June, representatives of twenty-four groups met to discuss the coalition. Discussion continued, although conflicting reports were received—of the coalition's demise, and of its plans for the future.

The August 26th women's demonstrations were a ritual activity that linked feminist groups and individuals.

The first August 26th demonstration was announced by Friedan at a NOW conference in the spring of 1970. Designed to commemorate the 50th anniversary of women's suffrage, the demonstration included women all over the country, who marched, demonstrated, and picketed. (The event included a well-publicized march in New York City.) A wide range of feminist groupings and individuals participated. Despite the fact that planning was marked by controversy over demeanor, activities, and ideological focus, the demonstration was held annually from 1970 through 1972, with a large spectrum of women's movement groupings participating.

Units in a segmentary system differ on means, goals, and method of operation. In the women's movement the New York City feminist groupings working on the issue of abortion before the liberalized New York State abortion law was passed in 1970 differed on means (lobbying, giant rallies, street petitions, procuring illegal abortions), on goals (reform of abortion laws, repeal of all laws relating to abortion, a new society where men would be deprived of power to make laws about women's bodies), and on group structure (from small, disciplined collectives to somewhat amorphous groupings specializing in dramatic "zap" actions, to a large, structured hierarchical organization). Nevertheless, these groups worked together on occasion, considered themselves part of the same social movement, and, working independently, achieved significant changes in both attitudes and laws regarding a woman's right to get an abortion.

Reticulation. The connection between units in segmentary social movements can be compared to a net, with lines crossing and intercrossing. As opposed to the traditional wheel form, where links radiate outward from a central leader, this type of network has no central linkages. Among the ways in which individuals and groups are linked in the feminist network are:

1. *Multiple membership.* Many women are active in more than one movement group. A number of New York femi-

nists, for example, belong to NOW and to more radical feminist groups. Although they disagree with some NOW policies, these women believe certain goals can best be pursued by a large national organization. Again, feminists who participate in a women's liberation action group may also belong to a consciousness-raising group with no direct tie to the action group.

2. *Friendship.* Many feminists have friends who are active in various groupings. A friend may be invited to attend a particularly interesting meeting or activity, the friend's group may be notified and may join the first group for a project. If social networks were graphed, with individuals represented by nodes and links shown by lines, some individuals would exhibit an exceptionally large number of connecting lines radiating from them.[12] These are the "sociometric stars," women with ties to a large number of feminists and groupings.[13] Some sociometric stars are also "media stars," who act as spokeswomen for the movement to the outside world. A graph of the personal network of a media star such as Steinem or Friedan would show dense linkages within and outside the movement, since one of the functions of such individuals is to act as an interface between the movement and the outside world. Some media stars are leaders in the traditional sense of the word—such as Friedan, a founder of NOW. Others, such as Steinem and Atkinson, perceive themselves as "spokeswomen" and find the media imputation of leadership a handicap. Unlike Steinem, Atkinson, and Friedan, a number of sociometric stars within the movement are relatively unknown to the outside world. These women are mentioned in the feminist media, but ignored by the nonfeminist press. Among them are journalists, lesbians, and activists who have spent many years working for the movement. Such women may or may not function as spokeswomen, leaders, or theorists; what characterizes each is an extremely large personal network among movement participants.

One individual was extremely active in an organization to abolish all abortion laws, writing, lecturing, and recruiting. She also worked as an architect, presenting papers on the status of women in architecture. In addition, she compiled an annotated and frequently updated bibliography on women. This woman attended a meeting of a university women's liberation group to ask the group to join a pro-abortion federation of feminist groups. When participants discussed a letter to be sent to various New York City feminists asking for money to help extricate the group from serious financial difficulties, the visitor suggested approximately forty names, which she gave, with addresses and phone numbers, from memory, with comments on good prospects. More than half the women suggested by the visitor contributed money.

Large personal networks such as this help individuals and groups solve problems; mobilize groups for special projects; pass on information from one grouping to another; and recruit individuals who may be interested in working on one particular project but then, through the sociometric star, meet feminists interested in other questions and move from a limited interest in a specific problem to a wide-ranging feminist commitment. The more such personal networks are activated, the more they grow, linking individuals and groups throughout the women's movement.

3. *Conferences and ritual events.* Groupings may combine for a meeting, rally, or conference. Although such events may have instrumental functions, they also have a ritual function, affirming and renewing the solidarity of the group. Such an event involves planning meetings, where questions such as program, space utilization, and publicity are discussed. Personnel to handle these details must be found. Personal networks are activated to find participants in the event; women tell their friends about the planned activity; they visit groups and announce the event and ask for volunteers to help. The larger the planned event, the more networks and groups are activated. During the event women meet other

feminists; exchange information; learn about new groups, innovative tactics, projected activities. Many women's liberation conferences conclude with an all-woman dance. Informants have reported a deep sense of community and solidarity at such dances. The following is a quote from my field notes about the performance of a women's theater group:

> The last number was a "chant" . . . this culminated in dancing which women from the audience were invited to join, and did. This was all-female, no-partner dancing like that at Susan's party (a feminist Christmas party) with the same sort of sharp, yipping, orgiastic cries. The music was of near-professional quality; beautiful melodies. . . . I found it all very moving—there was a great communication of feeling—a sort of primary-process communication. . . . It wasn't the contents so much as the *intensity* that was moving. . . . At the end, when the women were dancing to the music, I really kind of wished I could get up and dance, too.

I did not join the dancing because my husband was present. An actress with the group later said that many women were embarrassed to join the dancing when the group performed for mixed-sex audiences and that there was far more audience participation when the performance was for women only. Women who have shared such experiences at a ritual event feel they have something in common; they are truly "sisters."

4. *Women's centers.* The centers link individuals and groupings. They provide information and advice by telephone, referring women to feminist groups, sources, and services, and frequently hold classes, conferences, formal and informal social events, and fund-raising events to keep the center operating.

Groups sometimes organize to form a new women's center. The Community of Women was planning an East Side center in Manhattan. Whether or not the projected center opens and has sufficient funds to continue operating, the efforts to raise funds and form a center link diverse individuals and groupings.

5. *Women's studies courses.* Women's movement participants are interested in the history of feminism and in political, psychological, and sociological theories on women. In addition, many feminists look for material to help them develop a "feminist analysis," and women's studies courses frequently are designed to facilitate such an analysis. Again, one encounters a feedback mechanism: planning meetings; contact with various groupings; fund-raising activities; then the course or courses, where linkages increase and newcomers are recruited.

6. *Social and recreational activities.* A Greenwich Village restaurant run by feminists was opened in 1972; it is small and intimate, and feminists joined friends and met friends' friends there. Men are not barred from this restaurant, but few were observed there. Lesbian bars serve a similar function on occasion. So do all-women parties, which many feminists hold.

7. *Publications and other media.* Feminist media form a communications network, discussing issues and opinions, announcing group projects and tactics, and informing women about conferences, demonstrations, and rallies. Again, fund-raising activities for such chronically near-bankrupt publications help create further links.

The decentralized, segmented network structure of the movement can lead to duplication of efforts; one group or individual can spend time searching for or setting up a project or service that may already exist nearby geographically but be distant in terms of network connections. Because of differing tactics, however, duplication of effort may give a greater chance of success, since one particular group's tactics—and even goals—may turn out in retrospect to have been better planned or conceived. Thus, Sarah Miller, who worked with women's liberation abortion groups for several years (see Appendix), later believed that it was the efforts of NOW, using pragmatic political methods, that influenced the liberalizing of New York's abortion laws.

Despite the fact that the utopian women's liberation groups generated publicity, facilitated abortions, and helped convince people of the necessity for liberalized laws, participants were unwilling to use the traditional political tactic of lobbying to secure legal reforms.

The decentralized (or "structureless") structure of the women's liberation *groups* can be a disadvantage when seeking an immediate, tangible political goal, or when opposing a group seeking such a goal. For example, in the spring of 1972, a well-organized campaign was mounted by Right-to-Life groups (which feminists believed was financed by the Catholic church) to repeal the liberalized New York abortion law. Busloads of Right-to-Lifers arrived at Albany, furnished with well-constructed arguments and color photographs of dead fetuses. Despite the fact that women's movement participants were aware of the magnitude of the threat, abortion activists had difficulty getting other feminists to write letters, make phone calls, go to Albany—in short, to follow the effective tactics of the Right-to-Lifers. With the exception of NOW, which had an established lobbying program and a newsletter informing members what, where, and how to protest, there were no centralized mechanisms for mobilizing women for extended effort. When the magnitude of the threat became clear, a number of women did write letters, phone the governor, and go to Albany. But the multigroup structure of the movement was a liability when direct, immediate, concerted action was required. Similar difficulties have been encountered in working for the Equal Rights Amendment.

The decentralized structure of the movement is an advantage on occasion, however, since variation is maximized, options are explored, and new solutions may be found for various problems. Decentralization maximizes experimentation, which may give a better chance of hitting on new solutions to problems. But it minimizes the possibility of long-term coordinated work toward (or against) specific goals.

Women's liberation groups, which disapprove of formal leadership, structure and the exercise of power, tend to operate in terms of short-term challenge and response. A challenge-and-response characteristic can be a source of strength, facilitating mobilization of a large group to meet a perceived opportunity or threat. But this characteristic can also be a source of weakness. An informant, describing the early days of a militant women's liberation action group, said: "The approach wasn't 'let's sit down and survey things and see what to do.' Instead, people would come in with the latest outrage, and we'd attack it." The group operated primarily in response to "outrages" or challenges. When few challenges present themselves, or if the challenges do not have an immediate personal appeal for participants, a group will have difficulty mobilizing participants.

In the absence of formal structure, fixed positions, and chain of command, the emotional appeal of an issue is frequently the sole determinant of how many women will work on it. Using this criterion, abortion was the feminist issue par excellence—especially before the liberalized law was passed. A woman's initial commitment to the abortion issue might be greater at first than her commitment to the women's movement, and she might work with the first abortion group she encountered, whether it was a women's rights or women's liberation group. The combination of danger (participants might be breaking the law) and intense need escalated commitment—to abortion and to feminism. Thus, many women who helped others procure abortions had undergone an abortion themselves, or had suffered the social and economic consequences of not finding an abortionist. Each horror story they heard, each woman who would have been forced to bear an unwanted child and/or undergo a forced marriage were it not for their efforts, mobilized participants and made them stronger opponents of a social system that allowed such events. Thus women who worked for abortion were not only mobilized, they were frequently radicalized. Starting as proabortionists, they frequently ended as staunch radical feminists. In addition to its radicalizing influence, abortion work had a direct and immediate emotional payoff: results were desperately needed and results were visibly achieved. Marriage and divorce law reform is an issue with similar appeal; many women working on it have undergone traumatic divorces, and groups that work on this issue frequently help women secure divorces. Some issues are more abstract, however; they lack an immediate emotional payoff. It may be difficult to get participants to work on these issues in any organization, no matter how structured. But in a decentralized women's liberation group in particular, such issues are more likely to get short shrift no matter what their theoretical and long-range significance.

The decentralized, multigroup structure of the women's movement does have great flexibility. Women who agree on only one issue—such as abortion—are able to find a congenial group and work on that issue without their profound disagreements on tactics, goals, and methods of operation splitting or paralyzing movement effectiveness. The groups all see themselves as feminist, they are all working on the same issue, each in its own way. Participants are free to "do their own thing." Units are free to fuse and refuse for various activities, without a rigid structure forcing those who disagree with an entire program and/or ideology out of the movement. New units can form to fill a particular "niche" when a need is perceived. With the exception of bureaucratically structured organizations such as NOW, where factionalism can lead to serious difficulties, conflict leads to further segmentation—or to the disappearance of one unit within the network—rather than harming the movement as a whole.[14]

There is another advantage to a multigroup structure, which Gerlach and Hine call "escalation of effort." [15] When a revolutionary group presents what are perceived as violent and unreasonable demands, these demands may dispose authorities to be receptive to the more moderate proposals of a reform group.

> The leader of a New York NOW committee on media told members how she had contacted an editor of *Time* magazine when she heard they were preparing an issue on the changing role of women. She was told that this was not a women's liberation issue. Nevertheless, she visited the editor, who was pleased and

surprised at how "reasonable" she and the issues she presented were. Some of the issues she discussed were presented in the *Time* article on women.

The issues raised by the NOW leader might not have appeared quite so reasonable to the *Time* editor if there had not been an implied comparison between them and the demands of utopian women's liberationists. Another advantage of the multigroup structure was illustrated at the same meeting:

> A new woman, attending her first NOW meeting, described job difficulties at a public relations firm, where she had lower salary and a less imposing title than men doing the same work. She said she had heard some women's liberation speakers at her public relations club, but she just couldn't identify with them: "They weren't my kind of people." But when the leader of the NOW committee spoke at the club, the informant found her "much easier to take" and started to think about joining NOW.

The diversity of women's movement groupings allows an individual to find a unit with a congenial approach and style. Many novices who are alienated by the demeanor and demands of utopian feminists may feel at home in a pragmatic reform group. After some years of feminist commitment, such women may find more extreme demands reasonable and even appealing.

Because the women's movement occurs in a complex society, it may appear that the multigroup structural model applies solely to such urban and sophisticated movements. When accounts of social movements in simpler societies are reexamined, however, it becomes apparent that many such movements were probably also characterized by a decentralized, reticulated, multigroup structure concealed on occasion by the observer's belief that only a hierarchical bureaucratic organization exhibits structure and that the rest is chaos or an imperfect approximation of the ideal model.[16]

When an observer uses a traditional centralized bureaucratic model of a social movement, diversity, conflict and change pose conceptual problems. With the processual multigroup model, on the other hand, it becomes clear that the units that compose a social movement can differ in almost every conceivable way, disagree on means, goals, and structure, and alter as they are being observed. The multigroup model poses a different problem: that of unity. We must inquire what holds a movement together when it lacks a centralized structure or charismatic all-powerful leaders.

Here, the concept of an informally organized interest group unified by a dominant symbolism is helpful. Cohen ranges political groups on a continuum: at one pole are highly formal (contractual) groups organized along rational bureaucratic lines; at the other pole are informal (normative) groups that use "symbolic strategies" to articulate group organization.[17] In this view, a dominant symbolic form can perform many of the organizational functions of an informally organized interest group.

I believe the informally organized women's movement is unified by such a dominant symbolic form, based on an opposition between "the women's way" and "the way men do things." In this central symbolism, women are contrasted with men, feminists with nonfeminists, "us" with "them." Although the symbolism is found in women's rights circles, it originated in the women's liberation branch of the movement. To explore this symbolism, in the next chapter I present a case study of a women's liberation group, examining contradictions between the women's liberation operating principles and the instrumental needs of a political group. In chapter 10 I examine the values on which these operating principles are based. I explore the values in the light of the concept of communitas and show how these beliefs provide a symbolism that unifies the informally organized women's movement.

9   Contradictions in a Women's Liberation Action Group: A Case Study

Chapter 3 presented a case study of a feminist group seeking personal change. We turn now to a study of an action group seeking social change. The earlier case study had an essentially linear structure: the women joined to raise their consciousness, and since the group was defined by participants as successful, the goal was gradually achieved. The present case study lacks this simple and satisfying linear form. Instead, it is based on a series of contradictions. These can be viewed as contradictions between the "ideal" and the "real," but that would be an oversimplification. They are more nearly contradictions between reach and grasp, between ideology and necessity, between actors' and observers' models of the same processes.

The women's liberation action group to be examined is located at an urban university. Despite the fact that any woman was free to come to as many or as few meetings as she wished, almost every participant who remained for more than one or two meetings had some connection with the university.

The first contradiction is between a prohibition against leadership and the need for it. Leadership posed a problem in the university action group because it was both censured and exercised.

Leadership, as such, was rarely discussed although participants did talk with disapproval of "elitism" and "taking a unilateral action." Nevertheless, at the weekly meetings a recruit might notice some unusual procedures that were connected with leadership. First, participants frequently took a great deal of trouble to arrange the group in a circle at the beginning of meetings. The need for a circle was not questioned; the women seemed to take it for granted that this was naturally the best way to arrange meetings. Then, when the meeting began, someone would pass a piece of paper around the room, and this became the agenda; whoever wanted to bring up a subject wrote it on the paper. Third, weekly meetings had no customary chairperson; there was frequently discussion about who would chair the meeting. Although the chairperson was supposed to volunteer, many women appeared reluctant to do so.

These procedures, which might bewilder a novice, would eventually seem quite logical as part of an organized attempt to avoid institutionalized leadership. For this purpose a circle has symbolic and actual advantages: symbolically, a circle has no head, all positions are equal, with the consequent intimation that all contributions from these equal positions will be equally valuable, and valued equally; in reality, a circle facilitates visibility and generalized interaction patterns, with participants encouraged to interact directly with one another, rather than interaction being mediated through a central figure. Similarly, an agenda passed around the room encourages any individual who wishes to express herself on any subject to do so. A rotating volunteer chairperson is another way to avoid stabilized leadership roles.

Leadership was censured, but the university group did have women who led others. One of the most important functions of such women was to help the group dispense with "leadership."

For example, certain women consistently took the responsibility of persuading other women to chair. Chairing the weekly meeting required control, flexibility, and political skill. A too controlling chair was criticized for being authoritarian; a laissez-faire one heard complaints about an overlong and chaotic meeting. It was a classic double-bind: the chair was damned if she led and damned if she did not. Despite the fact that chairing meetings was supposed, in part, to be a learning experience where women would develop new skills, it was, in fact, so unpleasant a task for those who lacked the skill or talent that a number of women consistently refused to volunteer.

The women who tried to recruit others to chair meetings were the ones who attempted to move the group into a circle:

> As one meeting began, participants were seated in two rows facing each other. One row sat on a raised shelf near the door; the other sat on chairs in front of the windows facing the door. As the meeting commenced, one woman interrupted the discussion to leave the raised shelf, sit herself on the floor, and loudly announce: "Come on now, everyone, let's move in closer on the floor, in a circle!" When asked why the people in chairs should not merely move in closer to the shelf, she replied in a joking tone of voice: "If you're a leader, you have to lead. So I'm leading. I'm moving in."

This woman was indeed leading, in attempting to shift the women from the shelf and chairs into a circle. This might be considered leadership-to-abolish-leadership, since there was a distinct difference between shelf and chair positions. The people who sat on the raised shelf near the door occupied what would be the teacher's position in a classroom, while those on chairs in front of the windows were placed where students might sit. The difference was sufficiently marked so that a new woman, who entered the empty room for her first meeting and sat on the shelf, felt uncomfortable until she shifted to the chairs facing the shelf. The shelf was a raised

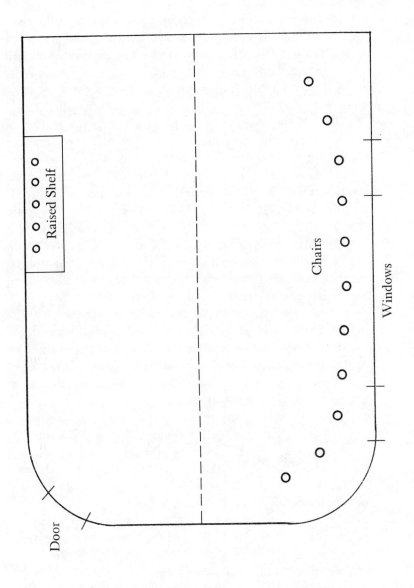

Figure 1. Room where action group meetings took place.

and exposed position; it just did not *feel* like the right place for a novice.

The difference between shelf and chairs was not discussed by participants. There was, however, a measurable difference in the amount of activity generated from the front-shelf half of the room as opposed to the chair half—even when the women were arranged in a circle, as they most frequently were.

I divided the room in two—the raised shelf in one-half of the room and the windows in the other half—noted where participants sat, and counted actions initiated during meetings. A formal action was defined as (1) sending the agenda around the room, (2) chairing the weekly meeting, and (3) writing a subject on the agenda, which the writer would discuss when the chair read the agenda item. There were twenty-nine weekly meetings of the university action group during the 1971–72 school year, of which I attended twenty-six. Four of these meetings had no agenda or chair. During the remaining twenty-two meetings, 211 actions were initiated from the shelf half of the room as opposed to 102 actions from the chair half, although an approximately equal number of people were seated in each half of the room. The Wilcoxon Matched Pair Sign Rank test indicates a significant difference between both halves of the room in amount of activity ($p \leq .01$). In addition, records were kept for twenty meetings on how many actions each person initiated: 95 women in the shelf half of the room initiated 187 actions, as opposed to 67 women initiating 89 actions in the window half. The Wilcoxon Matched Pair Sign Rank test shows a significant difference between halves of the room in amount of activity per person ($p \leq .05$).

The more active participants, then, tended to sit in the front of the room. Activity, of course, is not necessarily synonymous with leadership. With leadership, an act is *reciprocal:* a leader must have followers. And in the university group some women had followers, others did not.

The action group was proud of having no formalized leadership, structure, or chain of command. As a result, no one was able to delegate authority and assign others to work on a particular task. A project had to catch the interest of those willing to volunteer. Certain women were extremely successful in recruiting volunteers. These were the women other women followed. When they initiated a project, others were interested; when they requested volunteers, others volunteered. This ability to mobilize participants is particularly important in a "leaderless" group, where projects cannot be scheduled in advance because authority and work cannot be delegated. When no one at a meeting had the ability to mobilize others, volunteers were scarce, and few work details were organized for projects. Whenever this happened for a few consecutive weeks, projects faltered, the group became more "social" and less "instrumental," and many women began to skip meetings, complaining that the group was accomplishing little. Without leadership, then, a "leaderless" group might become increasingly inactive and might even stop functioning.

Although chairing the weekly action-group meetings was voluntary, certain individuals were most likely to be asked by others to chair larger meetings, where group participants joined with others. The same women frequently acted as spokeswomen when the group was involved with outside organizations or authorities. Although a "spokeswoman" was clearly and consciously differentiated from a "leader" by the group, she was usually perceived as "someone in charge" by authorities and media representatives. This was reinforced by the fact that such women handled themselves well; hesitant women were not selected to represent the group in public situations.

These spokeswomen frequently made a point of how frightened they were, of how they had to take a tranquilizer or a drink before a meeting to give them courage. "That was a two-tranquilizer, three-drink affair," said one woman after a television interview about a group project. Whether the tranquilizers and liquor were in fact necessary, the demurrers were, indicating that the spokeswoman was executing a painful duty and that she was as frightened and overcome as any rank-and-file participant.

Although everyone showed reluctance to characterize such

women as leaders (except during a dispute, when the description was an insult), these women filled leadership functions absolutely necessary for the success of projects and for group survival.

The leaders were intelligent, hard-working, and deeply committed. They volunteered for unpleasant tasks when no one else would, and stimulated others to volunteer. They initiated projects, encouraged timid women, solved problems, facilitated decision making. In return for these considerable efforts, they had a close circle of friends with whom they worked for a cause in which they believed intensely. They had a sense of purpose and, frequently, of accomplishment. They learned skills, tested and proved themselves in situations of conflict and crisis.

But leaders were also exposed to pointed remarks, barbed jokes, and on occasion outright hostility. Not only her behavior, but even a leader's ability might be termed "elitist." This leads to our second contradiction, between a belief in self-actualization and a definition of equality that penalizes superior ability.

> During a factional dispute in the university group, one woman accused another of being too verbal, too rational, of putting across her viewpoint with such power and brilliance that she "oppressed other women."
>
> The accuser said, "What the women's movement is about is getting rid of hierarchy and oppression. Some people always talk more at our meetings than others and that's wrong." She indicated that although the first woman was willing to share her skills and teach others, she had to "learn to be part of the group, just a member like all the others."
>
> The accused woman said: "I'm twenty-nine years old and I've been put down by men all my life for my brains and aggressiveness. What the women's movement is about is not to put down other women. I am

not competitive and I will not be put down by other women. I haven't led this year.... Why should I be put down for elitism? I've had that all my life—that's why I went into the women's movement."

Another participant, who talked little at meetings, said to the accused: "But you're so verbal and expressive that it makes it hard for women like me to talk. I find myself agreeing with you even when inside I know I disagree, because I can't put my objections into words, and I'm always interrupted, or people talk against me so strongly. Can't you say a little less so it would be easier for people like me to say a little more?"

The accused woman later said that she felt the group relied upon her brains and verbal ability in times of conflict, especially conflict with men. But when there were no men to feel oppressed by, then *she* was accused of oppressing other women.

The discussion between the two women was characterized by a complete incomprehension of what the other was saying—as though each were speaking a different language. This incomprehension may have resulted from the fact that the two were referring to conflicting feminist principles. To the accuser, feminism was associated with an egalitarian and antileadership ethic so radical that even differences in ability were perceived as hierarchical. The accused woman, on the other hand, believed feminism should encourage women to actualize their potential.

The first woman's conception of feminism was associated with a principle I shall call *radical egalitarianism*. In this view, individuals are seen as having equal potential, with differences in performance reflecting not differences in competence but in socialization. Since inequalities are believed to be the result of differential socialization, a feminist group has the responsibility of attempting to eliminate the effect of these inequities. One way to eliminate their effect is to abolish fixed leadership roles, since groups with leaders are hierarchical and hierarchy is believed to suppress the initiative of the majority of the membership.

Superiority, then, is unequal and hierarchical, as is leadership, because the superior ability of one individual is seen as blocking similar development among others (who are believed to have equal potential although they have not been given a chance to cultivate it).

In addition to leadership and ability, *training* was on occasion discussed as hierarchical in the university group. The woman who had accused the other of oppression had dropped out of college to do clerical work and support radical student organizations. She frequently intimated that the worries of other women about their classwork were selfish and hierarchical, since an education would put them in a privileged position vis-à-vis "ordinary working women." In the same spirit, a paper presented at a Feminist Psychology Conference asserts that *all* relationships between "professional" and client are hierarchical and oppressive, even when the professional considers herself a feminist: ". . . a woman who 'treats' another woman is not her sister. Not if the 'treatment' is psychotherapy with its hierarchy and interpretation. Not even if the treatment is more narrowly medical, when it includes the assumption of doctor-patient status differences." [1]

Radical egalitarianism perceives the traditional relationship between male and female, white and black, professional and client, teacher and student, leader and follower as unequal, hierarchical, and oppressive. This view can lead to a vulnerability to, or even a predilection for, being treated, advised, helped, and taught by those with few or questionable qualifications. Thus, one participant in the university group was overheard chiding another for seeking a psychotherapist with a medical background.

The accused woman in the dispute associated feminism with self-realization, with being allowed to develop herself as an individual instead of being forced into a constricting "feminine" role. Self-development is a feminist principle (as is radical egalitarianism), and action-group members took pains to help others learn new skills. The institution of rotating chair, for example, was intended to teach those who lacked experience in conducting a meeting how to do so, the implication being that men were routinely taught such skills while women needed to learn them. Great effort was expended to involve new university-group participants in activities, to give them responsibility, to draw them into a core of activist women.

> A novice almost accidentally attended a subcommittee meeting of a special action group. She subsequently received a phone call inviting her to another committee meeting, and then a call asking for help at a press conference. The recruit was then asked to help a leader write a letter to the university chancellor. The novice sat while the leader drafted a letter, and agreed when asked to let her name be used as one of three group representatives the chancellor could contact. The leader then requested that the new woman place the press conference on the agenda of the weekly action group meeting and describe what happened. After the weekly meeting, the recruit was asked by the leader to be interviewed on the subject for a radio program. The novice was bewildered by the issues, which involved two years of work by participants, and wondered why someone more expert was not called in.

It gradually became evident to the novice that it was unacceptable for one person or small group to be identified in the action group as "experts" or specialists. This led to a quality one might call "permeability"—new women found themselves actively assimilated into meetings, crises, decisions, responsibilities. As they were assimilated into the group, novices were encouraged to develop new skills.

But self-development can be an ambiguous principle in a collective context, since differentiation may be perceived as a threat to the collectiveness of the group. One finds an implication in many women's liberation groups that achievement and ability endanger the group and must be curbed—or the achiever thrust from the group. A feminist theater director described this in a speech where she told why she was leaving the women's movement:

> If you are in the first category, an achiever, you are immediately labeled a thrill-seeking opportunist, a ruthless mercenary, out to get her fame and fortune over the dead bodies of selfless sisters who have buried their abilities and sacrificed their ambitions for the greater glory of Feminism. Productivity seems to be the major crime—but if you have the misfortune of being outspoken and articulate, you are accused of being power-mad, elitist, fascist, and finally the worst epithet of all: A MALE IDENTIFIER, AAARRGG!! [2]

Connected with a bias against achievement, ability, and expertise is the accusation of "ripping off the movement," a criticism frequently leveled against those who have received publicity or success for women's movement activities. The implication is that such women are using the movement for personal gain, and feminists who establish a successful—or even viable—enterprise are besieged with requests for free services from feminist groupings and individuals, services that might, if fulfilled, destroy the enterprise.

> Kate Millett made a feminist film, for which she charged a rental that was difficult for women's liberation groups to meet, since such groups tend to be chronically short of funds. The university action group was one of many that asked if Millett would waive the rental fee so they could show the film to raise money for a special project; Millett, on the other hand, wanted to make enough money from the film to pay the actresses and film crew, who had donated their services.

Representatives of groups Millett turned down were heard on occasion expressing resentment. And in 1974, the *Village Voice* reported that the women who helped Millett make the film were suing her for a share of the proceeds. It was a double-bind, no-win situation.

Depicting successful feminists as ripping off the movement, or forcing a gifted individual from a group, are extreme manifestations of a definition of self-development that sees women as less developed than men because of differential socialization, and then classifies more developed women as oppressive and hierarchical—like men.

Two contradictions have been examined: between a women's liberation prohibition against leadership and a need for it; and between an ideal of individual self-realization and a principle of radical egalitarianism that perceives differences in ability as hierarchical. Linked to the belief that leadership and superior ability are hierarchical is a ban on the exercise of power; power, too, is believed to be oppressive (and masculine). A third related contradiction can be explored—between a principle of nonstructure and the way in which the university group actually functioned.[3]

The women's liberation model of group structure is the consciousness-raising group, and lack of formal structure is stressed as a way of discouraging hierarchy and power. Participants in the university action group spoke of it as leaderless and unstructured: "We're a very organic group," said one woman, asking new participants to suggest group projects they wanted to work on. I have described group mechanisms to rotate or abolish leadership functions and sanctions applied to those who appeared too able or aggressive. These are primarily negative practices, however, to *abolish* hierarchy and *discourage* leadership and the exercise of power. How, then, did anything get done? Who decided what to do, and who did it?

As shown, some women were significantly more active in the group than others, and these women tended to sit in front of the room during meetings. This "core" of activists, which included but was not limited to leaders, did most of the work. There was an active friendship network operating among these core women. Most activists lived near the university and worked or attended classes there. Core women saw one another frequently for planned and informal activities.

A member of this central core kept a diary for a week during the school year, noting all informal contacts with other members:

> The informant had thirty-seven contacts with group participants during the week—an average of five a day (plus the participants she saw at the weekly action-group meeting and at the meeting of her consciousness-raising group). Of these: 10 contacts occurred by telephone; there were 10 more or less planned meetings with 16 women; and 9 unplanned meetings. Action-group projects were discussed at 13 of these 29 calls and meetings; 6 meetings were devoted to "news" or "general women's stuff"; 8 appeared to have been primarily social, although action group news may have been discussed; and 6 were concerned with interpersonal aid, such as borrowing an automobile or getting advice about a student loan.

> During the week of the diary, the informant had three dinners and two lunches with other participants. In addition, she spent one evening at a meeting of her consciousness-raising group, which was sponsored by the action group, and attended the weekly action-group meeting another evening. Thus, the informant spent all or part of five evenings that week with other action-group members. During that time group activities were discussed, ideas and information exchanged, and personal help offered and accepted.

The active women tended to sit together during meetings. This was probably due less to exclusiveness than to the fact that as friends, they had much to talk about. Friendship ties were important in facilitating projects: friends would volunteer for one another's projects—especially if they knew someone was hard-pressed; a friend might support another's position during a dispute—or feel free to disagree vociferously with a particular stand, feeling this would not affect the friendship. Women who did not belong to this central friendship network were more timid about expressing disagreement. Some links within the friendship network were based upon common membership in consciousness-raising groups the previous year; the women who had been in groups together tended to see one another socially and offer help to one another when necessary. Other ties were based on personal magnetism. Some leaders were "sociometric stars" with exceptionally large personal networks of social relations; these women had followers, who tended to come to meetings, volunteer for work details, and become involved with projects when the leader did so.

The structure of this "structureless" group consisted, then, of a well-connected central network of friends, with friendship ties replacing a chain of command in helping to mobilize and activate participants. In addition to the central group, each member of the core had personal friendship networks that could be activated when personnel was needed. The people in these individual networks included women who attended meetings but were not particularly active, those who attended few meetings but could be recruited for special projects, and women who were linked to the activator rather than the group but could be mobilized for aid on occasion.

A former member wrote of the university group:

> One very important feature . . . was the strong friendships that developed between women in the group . . . which had as an important component the idea of *doing something* that you said you would do

by a certain time, and in fact did do, since others were dependent on you to do it. . . .[4]

The working structure of this "structureless" group was based, then, on a central core of friends with participants activated by friendship, loyalty, and a feeling of working together for a common cause.

Another factor helped activate participants: a sense of crisis, of emergency, a feeling that if a particular task was not completed by a specified time, something terrible would happen. The core woman worked day and night, weekends and holidays. Driven by this urgency, participants would schedule meeting after meeting; these would be long and frequently inconclusive. Meetings often broke up late at night with little decided, and another meeting would then be scheduled for the following evening or weekend. Work details labored evenings and weekends on leaflets, letters, press releases, and plans for larger meetings.

Despite the fact that participants appeared to perceive the meetings and work details as a *response* to the sense of urgency, I believe the effort and interaction helped create the feeling of emergency to which they were ostensibly responding.

One reason that meetings were long, inconclusive, and frequently scheduled was that decision making posed a problem similar to that of leadership. Although decisions were necessary, there was a belief that these should be "group decisions." [5]

A novice received a phone call at 11:30 P.M. from two action-group members who were working on leaflets announcing a rally planned at the previous weekly action group meeting. The caller advanced reasons why the scheduled rally date was unwise, and asked the recruit's approval for placing a different date on the leaflet.

The novice became used to receiving late-night phone calls

asking her to approve of last-minute decisions. The phone calls helped validate such rulings as group decisions.

Taking "a unilateral action" was regarded with such disapproval among participants that I was unable during one crisis period to discover who had decided to call a particular emergency meeting. The request for information was construed as criticism, and the reaction of informants was so defensive that questioning had to be dropped.

The university group utilized a decision-making technique that might be called "decision by exhaustion." This was in line with the high value placed on consensus in the group and the conscious avoidance of formal structure, including the avoidance of special roles and mechanisms to facilitate decision making. This technique had some interesting consequences, which influenced the group's "working structure," as opposed to its formal structure—or "structurelessness."

"Planning meetings" to make specific decisions tended to be long and inconclusive. Individuals who disagreed took turns to repeat their point of view, over and over, as though repetition would lead to eventual consensus. Such a meeting would break up late at night with little decided, and another meeting would be scheduled. And another. For example:

Seven preliminary planning meetings for a confrontation between the action group and the university chancellor were counted—followed by an eighth meeting to discuss the confrontation. The following is a list of preliminary planning meetings, their duration, the number of participants, and decisions taken. (The content of five of the seven meetings was recorded.)

1. Date: Friday evening, February 11
    Participants: 4 women (plus outside feminist
    lawyer asked to help)
    Duration: (not known)
    Decisions: To hold faculty meeting on subject on
    February 18.

2. Date: Sunday, February 13, 4:00 P.M.
   Participants: 8 women, 1 man (husband)
   Duration: 3 hours, 15 minutes
   Decisions: Agreed on agenda for meeting to be
   held the next day.

3. Date: Monday, February 14, at noon
   Participants: 9 women
   Duration: 2½ hours
   Decisions: Two demands proposed for confronta-
   tion.

4. Date: Monday evening, February 14
   Participants: 8 women
   Duration: 4 hours
   Decisions: Previous two proposals dropped, five
   new demands formulated.

5. Date: Tuesday, February 15
   Participants: (not known)
   Duration: (not known)
   Decisions: Agenda drawn for faculty meeting next
   day. Dispute about five demands of
   Monday evening. New suggestions.

6. Date: Wednesday, February 16, at noon
   Participants: 36 women (11 action-group participants, 23 faculty members, 2 college
   students)
   Duration: 2½ hours
   Decisions: Preliminary suggestions for university-
   wide plan on issue. (Another meeting
   of faculty scheduled to produce leaflet
   and work independently on issue.)

7. Date: Wednesday, February 16, 4:00 P.M.
   Participants: 11 women (including feminist
   lawyer)
   Duration: 1 hour
   Decisions: Refinement of proposals advanced in
   fifth meeting and adaptation of another demand, suggested at sixth meet-

ing. Five demands agreed upon to
present to chancellor.

Confrontation

Date: Wednesday, February 16, 5:00 P.M.
Participants: 11 women (same women as at meet-
ing 7)
Duration: 1½ hours
Decisions: Five demands presented, and second
meeting with chancellor scheduled.

8. Date: Wednesday, February 17, 6:30 P.M.
Participants: 11 women (same as at meeting 7 and
confrontation)
Duration: (not known)
Decisions: Discussion and preparation of press
release on confrontation. Planning
meeting for second confrontation
scheduled.

During the first meeting, the decision was made to
hold a faculty meeting to involve female faculty in
the issue. During the second meeting the idea of
using the confrontation to make demands that the
chancellor could meet or ignore, rather than global
demands and complaints, was formulated. Demands
were proposed during the third meeting. These were
vetoed, with new demands substituted during the
fourth meeting. The new demands were discussed
and disputed with new proposals advanced during the
fifth meeting. During the sixth meeting an entirely
new group of women proposed demands and other
possible actions. The final decision on what demands
to present was made during a one-hour meeting just
before the confrontation. There was a time limit on
this sixth meeting, since the confrontation was scheduled for an hour later.

The first reaction of an observer who sees eight meetings,
involving more than fourteen hours during six days, may well

be that this is incredibly inefficient. Time and effort appear to be used in such a prodigal manner that it seems remarkable that such a group is able to accomplish anything. If decision making was the sole reason for these meetings, one might wonder whether two meetings—one to suggest ideas and one for final decisions—might not be adequate.

Further observation would indicate, however, that despite occasional grumbling, the women appeared relatively satisfied with this method of operation. In fact, participants did not appear to be aware of exactly how decisions came about. Decisions were necessary, one had planning meetings, and eventually decisions occurred. What was discussed among participants was how *not* to make decisions—"unilateral decisions" were censured; leaders spoke with concern of how "we mustn't have a small group of people taking over," and an accusation of "elitism" could paralyze a leader, a planning meeting, or an entire project.

This method of decision making seemed to avoid elitism, unilateral decisions, and power vested in a small group. The fact that so many meetings were held meant that anyone interested in an issue could attend at least one meeting, offer an opinion, and have it considered and on occasion adopted, even if the proposal lasted for only one or two more meetings before being replaced by another proposal. By the time the final decisions were agreed upon, so many proposals had been discussed so many times that it was difficult to remember exactly who had decided what. The numerous meetings helped obscure the decision-making process, so that resolutions were transformed into "group decisions"—with general haziness about who had proposed and decided what.

Decision by exhaustion, then, was (or was perceived to be) decision by consensus.

In addition, the proliferation of meetings helped create a sense of urgency and crisis, which had an important integrating function. The tension, effort, and fatigue of days and nights spent working against an emergency deadline—and each meeting was pervaded with a sense of time pressing upon participants—drew participants closer.

There was a feeling of intense closeness between those who shared this sense of crisis. The small group had pushed itself past fatigue, sacrificed evenings and weekends to work on a cause that, because of this effort, became more important and meaningful. *One experienced the sisterhood for which one was working.* And since the goal was conceptualized as one of sisterhood, of extending sisterhood into a political program and way of life, the struggle validated the goal.

It is pertinent to note here that a feeling of shared struggle could mask a number of important differences. The political goals and personal styles of participants might vary significantly, so much so that rational discussion of exactly what the group was working for might lead to dissension. But the work, the struggle, and the fatigue fused a disparate group and forged powerful emotional links. The women had been on the barricades together; they had shared something very important.

The sense of emergency was dependent upon having an enemy. The "we" of the group required a "they" against whom the group united. Gerlach and Hine note the importance of opposition in increasing participation and escalating commitment.[6] Unless we understand this function of opposition, the university action group's attitude toward the administration might appear exaggerated. The eight planning meetings discussed above were concerned with a confrontation with the university chancellor, who was perceived as a man of prodigious intelligence, cunning—and bad faith. The chancellor was the embodiment of "them"—a powerful and dangerous force against which one must unite or be destroyed. An outside observer might wonder whether any one individual could exhibit the brilliant, powerful duplicity attributed to the chancellor. Should the observer get caught up in the struggle, however, this view would appear not only logical but also inevitable; this is the way "they" were, and the chancellor exemplified the characteristics the action group was opposing. Of course the chancellor made promises and broke them. Naturally he denied making statements one had heard him utter. Certainly he said one thing and then did the opposite. This is the way "they" behaved—and that was why the group had to battle against "their" arbitrary power.

The proliferation and length of meetings not only helped make decisions (and transform them into group decisions) and create and amplify a sense of emergency, but also acted as an extrusion mechanism. The meetings devoured time—as did the innumerable tasks associated with special action-group projects. Among the tasks that work details had to be formed for were: telephoning women to ask for help, and to announce meetings and demonstrations; writing, stenciling, and mimeographing leaflets, then distributing them on campus; writing notices and posting them on campus; passing petitions; collecting money on campus with a cardboard box; writing ads for the campus newspaper announcing meetings and rallies, then delivering them to the paper with payment; drawing posters to be carried in demonstrations; speaking in public at protest meetings and demonstrations and persuading others to do so; writing letters to newspapers about an issue; scheduling press conferences, arranging for speakers, statements, and the like; delivering press statements to New York City newspapers and television stations. Participation in these activities was on a volunteer basis; any woman who wished to take part did so. But those who could not volunteer felt guilty. And those who lacked the time to work on special projects would remain on the periphery of the group—or drop out. During a weekly action-group meeting, one woman spoke to a group activist who frequently requested volunteer aid:

> "I know you get angry at me because I don't help more," she said. "But you don't understand. I have three children. I have to prepare three meals a day and clean the toilets. I'm responsible for four human beings and it weighs on me. I take on one-shot jobs where I can work hard for a short period of time and then stop. I just don't have the time to help as much as I'd like. Sometimes I feel so badly about it that I say I'll come or help when I know I can't."

The sense of urgency and crisis, of the supreme importance of the task that united the women who worked together, excluded those who could not join in. Shared effort amplified commitment, but those with other commitments might not be able to share the effort. It might be difficult for a serious student, teacher, or regularly employed woman to attend so many meetings and work details. If she had a husband and/or children, her difficulties were compounded. Even a weekly consciousness-raising group meeting might cause an individual to miss "important" emergency meetings or work details.

> A university instructor said she had stopped coming to action-group meetings, although interested in the issues, because of the frequency of emergency meetings and requests for help. "Look," she said, "I'm teaching and writing my dissertation, and my husband and I take turns caring for the baby. It's just not fair to ask him to spend extra time with the baby while I go to all these meetings!" Although this woman was interested in the instrumental goals of the group, she did not have time (or need) for the expressive goals.

Participants frequently expressed distress that many women attended a few weekly action-group meetings and then dropped out. They discussed ways of attracting more faculty members, more young mothers, more people interested in working for child care on campus. They did not seem to be aware that an extrusion mechanism was operating, which tended to push out individuals with other commitments. Active participants started with few commitments, or their outside commitments were attenuated as group interaction increased. For example, two women attended all eight meetings discussed above; one attended seven; two attended six. The two women who attended all the meetings, and the one who attended seven meetings, were unmarried; none had a relationship with a man; none was a full-time student; all lived near the campus. Of the two women who attended six meetings, one was doing fieldwork for her dissertation and although married and with children, she had full-time household help. The second woman was also married, with children, and had come to the university action group for help in getting reinstated to a university job from which she had been fired; her job was one of the issues the confrontation concerned. In addition, this woman's mother lived with her family and helped with household tasks and child care. In short, a married woman with children could not have kept up with the meetings and work details without exceptional motivation—and household help.

Theoretically, a married woman with children, whose household responsibilities kept her from doing some of the things she might like to do, should have particular sympathy for women's liberation goals. But sympathy differs from the day-to-day process of interaction and commitment. One could become part of the close-knit central core only by experiencing the camaraderie of the evening and weekend emergency meetings. A woman with outside responsibilities might have difficulty doing this. And if she were not part of the core, the commitment that was fed by interaction might lag. Commitment, then, although frequently conceptualized in terms of an ideology, was in actuality commitment to the small group; women who could not meet the group's extensive demands for time moved to its periphery and, on occasion, left the group.

In addition to the time demands posed by the proliferation of meetings and work details, there was a second extrusion mechanism in the group—some women simply were not invited to join the core group. Freeman compares recruitment to the elite core of a women's liberation group to being pledged for a sorority, and notes that the individual has to "fit in" to join the inner circle.[7]

A woman who is not recruited to the core group will feel lonely and out of things. A novice might make friends through her action-group-sponsored consciousness-raising group, and then become part of a network that includes core women. But not everyone from a consciousness-raising group is recruited. A woman who did not have personal friends in the action group might find it difficult to keep attending meetings. She would be excluded from the informal conversational groupings that clustered before the weekly meetings began. The places near her might remain empty during a meeting. Participants might converse while she gave an opinion, or listen politely and then ignore what she said. When a group of women went to eat at a restaurant after the weekly meeting, they might not invite her, or she might be invited in an extremely careful, "kind" manner. It is hard for all but the most dedicated, insensitive, or aggressive woman to survive such treatment. A woman who did not fit in and make personal friends would be frozen out.

I discovered this, in a very personal way, during my second year with the university action group. Although by this time a veteran member, I started to feel extremely uncomfortable at meetings and found I was looking for excuses to avoid group meetings. It gradually became clear that the discomfort was related to the fact that I was "unpopular," that I was avoided and not particularly liked by those in control of the group. It then became apparent that I had been "popular" the previous year; I had been sought out and had many friends and companions in the group. The first year, I was "sponsored" by a group leader, who drew me into activities and sought my help and advice. But the composition of the group had changed. During the first year, there were more older students and more heterosexual women among core members; during the second year, there were more undergraduates and more bisexual and overtly homosexual women. Attending meetings was a pleasure the first year and an ordeal the second. I probably would have left the group the second year if it had not been part of my dissertation research.

Because the group operated through informal friendship networks, whose members were not selected by conscious overt criteria, participants did not appear to comprehend the way in which these extrusion mechanisms operated. There was much discussion about welcoming new women and, on occasion, special time periods would be set aside for that activity. One could schedule time to be friendly with new women, but one could hardly order active participants to make friends with all recruits. This was seen as a private, personal activity.

As a consequence of the two extrusion mechanisms, although any woman was free to attend meetings, and many did (including university instructors, professors' wives, neighborhood women, students, university employees, and assorted waifs and strays), those who remained formed a comparatively homogeneous close-knit group. Some individuals managed to form casual friendships with a few women, devote limited time to group activities, and remain on the periphery of the group, to be mobilized for large "actions." The core women, however, interacted frequently and with intensity. Group structure was based upon these core women, and group leaders came from this nucleus.

This case study of a women's liberation action group is based on contradictions between actors' and observer's models of group functioning. Members wished the group to follow certain principles and appeared to believe that, by and large, it did so. Observed behavior, however, indicated that these principles were violated as often, if not more often, than they were obeyed and that, in fact, the principles might be impossible to follow.

These contradictions have been called oppositions between the way participants appeared to believe the group functioned (the actors' model) and the behavior observed by the anthropologist (observer's model). They might also be viewed as confusions between means and end. Women's liberation ideology is based on certain principles—self-actualization, radical egalitarianism, consensus decision making, and a ban on leadership, structure, and the exercise of power. These are perceived as means, or operating principles. The goal of women's liberation, however, is to create a revolution, and although these operating principles are perceived as an integral part of the revolution to come (they are ends as well as means), they can, in fact, conflict or interfere with the achievement of that revolution.

About the Action Group

Data for this case study came from two years of participation in weekly group meetings, special committee meetings, fission into special-cause organizations, rallies, confrontations, emergency actions, work details, consciousness-raising groups, and outside socialization among participants.

A questionnaire was filled out by twenty-one women who had attended three or more group meetings during the 1971–72 school year. Two were college students; four were attending night college; and six were Ph.D. candidates. Respondents could fill in more than one occupation: thirteen listed themselves as students; four were university teachers, three secretaries, two "revolutionaries" (both belonged to the Socialist Workers' party), two university administrators, one editor, and one journalist. All had some connection with the university, including students, former students, employees, former employees, and faculty wives. Nine women said their "religious background" was Jewish (four of these indicated they had no present religious beliefs); eight came from Protestant backgrounds (five indicated no present religious beliefs); and three had been raised as Catholics (all three indicated no present religious beliefs). Eleven women were single, seven were married, one was separated, and two indicated ambiguous marital situations. The seven married women lived with their husbands; one unmarried respondent lived with a man; four, with several women; five, alone; two, with mixed-sex groups. Three participants had one child each; of these, one lived with her child and several women, the other two lived with husband and child. One participant had three children, was separated from her husband, and lived with the children. Of the husbands and ex-husbands, four were university professors, two lawyers, one a business executive, one a sculptor. (One respondent, who lived alone, indicated that she was or had been "all but married" to a film maker; another, who lived with her child and several women, had a relationship with a printer—she wrote "Other" when asked whether she was single, married, divorced, or separated.) Thirteen women said they were heterosexual; four, bisexual; one, homosexual; and four gave ambiguous responses when questioned on their sexual orientation. Two respondents were "revolutionary socialists"; seven called themselves "radical" or "left" or both; one was "left-feminist"; two were "left-Democrat"; and two indicated mixed political views. All considered themselves feminists.

10

The Symbolism of
Women's Liberation

I have shown how the operating principles of a women's liberation group included radical egalitarianism; self-actualization; group decision making; and a ban on leadership, structure, and the individual exercise of power. During the time of my observation, these principles were rarely discussed; they seemed to be taken for granted. What was discussed by participants were violations of these principles. Participants did not dwell on a prohibition against leadership and structure; they talked of "elitism" and how "a small group of women mustn't take over." Power was rarely discussed; instead, members talked of "the way women did things"—with an assumption that the way women did things was cooperatively—as opposed to the way men did things, which was coercively. Group decision making was not mentioned but "taking a unilateral action" was discussed with disfavor. Ability and expertise were on occasion condemned as hierarchical, and feminist professionalization discussed as "ripping off the movement."

Despite the fact that violations were censured and observed behavior differed from the operating principles, participants appeared to believe that these principles were generally followed.

These women's liberation operating principles may have been violated so frequently because they were unworkable. Although a small consciousness-raising group whose goal is self-expression and personal change may be able to dispense with leadership and structure, a group devoted to instrumental activity probably cannot, without also dispensing with the activity. If these women's liberation principles are essentially unworkable, as some commentators have stated,[1] why do they exist? Where do they come from?

Freeman explains the principles as "a natural reaction against the over-structured society in which most of us found ourselves, the inevitable control this gave others over our lives, and the continual elitism of the Left and similar groups."[2] Carden notes that they derive from ideas in the radical subculture and the more progressive elements in religion, education, the arts, and politics. Carden also indicates that many women's liberationists believe that changing to more traditional operating procedures would be adopting "an essentially masculine way of working."[3]

Here are a set of traits—egalitarianism; self-realization; sisterhood; cooperation; collectivism; a concern for personal experience; and a repudiation of power, hierarchy, and leadership—that are sometimes perceived as female characteristics as opposed to male. On other occasions they are regarded as prescribed behaviors rather than characteristics—they are the way a female (or a feminist) should behave. In addition, the traits are discussed as an end; this is the way everyone should behave, and will behave, when a feminist revolution is achieved.

The principles by which women's liberation groups operate, then, are not only principles for organizational procedures, but also *values*:

... highly generalized normative rules about what

kinds of honour or prestige a political actor should aim for, and equally generalized guides to the kind of conduct thought proper in the competition. Furthermore, behind these prescriptions lie existential propositions—ideas about human nature and the "natural" condition of human communities and the relation between man and nature.[4]

In saying that women's liberation groups are value-oriented, we imply that *they wish to effect basic transformations in such conceptions, and in relations based on them.* Norm-oriented groups, on the other hand, do not seek to alter basic conceptions; instead, they wish to enforce widely accepted conceptions.

I would like here to extend this discussion on values and the women's movement. My analysis is somewhat lengthy and may appear to take the reader a bit far afield. But I think it is important, and I hope its necessarily difficult content has been presented clearly.

The values, or new conceptions, advocated by women's liberation are always contrasted with their opposites. The opposing conceptions are described as "the way men do things," the way women who behave "like men" operate, and as the way our "patriarchal society" functions. Thus the opposite pole of radical egalitarianism, where all differences are to be erased, is hierarchy, where status differences are stressed. Self-actualization is contrasted with repression; sisterhood and cooperation with exclusion and coercion; personal experience with sterile abstraction; and collectivism with oppressive individualism.

The belief that men represent hierarchy while women represent a "community or even communion of equal individuals" is central to women's liberation.[5] I believe that this concept of communion, which has been called *communitas*, underlies and organizes women's liberation values. I shall examine the concept of communitas, show how it consists of a set of paired opposites, and describe the way in which women's liberation attempts to extend it from an experience into a set of rules for behavior and a blueprint for a new society.

The term *communitas* as used by the anthropologist Victor Turner can be understood only in terms of its opposites. Communitas is "antistructure" as opposed to "structure." Structure, in this usage, refers to a "society" or social structure composed of statuses, roles, and positions.[6] Within structure the individual is identified only by role; the social personality rather than the concrete feeling human being is important.[7] The concept of communitas is difficult to grasp because it is so connected to its opposite. Communitas is one half of a set of paired oppositions: egalitarianism as opposed to hierarchy; liminality or social marginality as opposed to a system of statuses; a timeless lack of differentiation as opposed to organization-within-time. The relation of communitas to its opposite pole resembles the Gestalt figure and ground; communitas is the ground, which is perceived only when juxtaposed against the figure.

> ... in communitas, social structure is suspended—group life is homogeneous and undifferentiated, therefore the whole woman matters. Her social roles do not. ... It is only when the whole woman is permitted to act spontaneously, without social responsibility and accountability, that communitas can develop. By definition, communitas cannot take place within structure, for it is ecstatic, literally an escape from the self. The spirit in soaring flight is liberated from the body and, correspondingly, from the social and historical rootedness that provides the daily mortal context.[8]

I have said that the concept of communitas is one half of a set of paired oppositions that is always perceived in juxtaposition to its opposite. The concept is further complicated by the fact that although communitas primarily refers to an experience, it is frequently extended by a group into a set of rules to guide behavior, and into a plan for a new utopian way of life.

First, let us examine the experience of communitas: here an individual leaves the fixed social structure to experience a joining, a merging, a communion, returning then to the everyday world of structure.[9] The experience is ecstatic and transforming; it is

> being no longer side by side (and one might add above and below) but with one another of a multitude of persons. And this multitude, though it moves towards one goal, yet experiences everywhere a turning to, a dynamic facing of the others, a flowing from *I* to *Thou*.[10]

A woman who becomes a feminist may experience for the first time this ecstatic sense of community with other women. There is the feeling of warmth, of belonging, of merging that can occur in a consciousness-raising group.[11] Communitas may be experienced at rallies and "actions," when a woman is marching with other women, surrounded by indifferent or hostile spectators; it may appear late at night when a small group of exhausted feminists is racing against a deadline to complete a project. This feeling of intense intimacy and trust, this "communion of mutually supportive women," can be an intoxicating experience.[12] It is an important aspect of the term *sisterhood*—when a feminist calls another woman "sister," a communion is implied. The communion excludes outsiders; it is believers against unbelievers, women against men, revolutionary feminists against the masculine power structure.

The experience of communitas adds richness and depth to female bonding. But this feeling appears to be perceived on occasions as more than an *experience;* it is discussed by feminists as a sex-linked set of traits and values. Men are believed to represent power and hierarchy; women represent sisterhood, solidarity, and community.

This association of women with communitas, and men

with its opposite, stems from (1) the attributes of the concept of communitas, (2) the structural position of women, and (3) certain characteristics of the traditional female role in our society.

Myerhoff, expanding upon Turner,[13] divides the modalities of social life into a set of oppositions: one pole represents communitas; the other, social structure and organization.[14] Despite the fact that these oppositions are derived from a comparison between the ideology and rituals of a tribe of Mexican Indians and those of counterculture American students, they illuminate women's liberation values. The list provided below is Myerhoff's, with certain items rearranged and "woman" substituted for "man" when appropriate. In addition, I have divided the list into two groups, with the second group presented in a footnote. Myerhoff's oppositions were generated by the experience of communitas. Since I shall consider communitas not only as *experience*, but also as a sex-linked characteristic, a set of rules for behavior, and a blueprint for a utopian society, the first set of oppositions is more appropriate for these extensions of the concept.

Liminality/Communitas/ Ecstasy *	*Social Structure/Status System/Organization*
social homogeneity, equality	hierarchy, differentiation
involvement of the total woman	partial man, in status positions, playing roles
sexual relations diffuse and outside monogamy and nuclear family	sexual relations focused, confined to marriage and family
concrete, immediate, direct relations among women, with nature and supernatural	attenuated and indirect relations

---

* At the bottom of the next page is the remainder of Myerhoff's oppositions, which is more relevant to the *experience* of communitas (which she discusses) than to the attempt to institutionalize communitas:

moral superiority manifested by structural inferiority	moral superiority manifested by structural superiority
absence of distinguishing insignia, disregard for dress and personal appearance, indicators of rank; preference for uniforms or undistinguished garments	concern with distinctions, personal appearance, external manifestations of achievement and prestige
stress on simplicity and the natural in dress; relations to the natural world highly stressed	complexity, artifice, "cultured" and "civilized" attenuated relations to the natural world stressed

The belief that communitas is the property of a particular group is not new. Similar phenomena have been described for movements among other social and religious groups, including students,[15] counterculture people,[16] Black Power participants, and Pentecostalists.[17] Women's liberationists attribute

Liminality/Communitas/ Ecstasy	Social Structure/Status System/Organization
value on transition, flow, continuity	stasis, permanence, bounded, discrete
freedom, lack of responsibility to others, ecstasy, loss of self, pleasure	restraint, self-control, duty, delayed gratification
value on unpredictability, uncertainty, ambiguity, and danger	value on predictability, certainty, regularity, clarity, and safety
time- and place-free; future treated as open-ended, unknowable, or nonexistent; past as irrelevant	time and place bound; orientation to a known past and knowable future
mystical powers, intuition, the innate as a source of authority and knowledge; distrust of intellectual, verbal, cognitive, rational, analytic systems	distrust of mystical, intuition, innate as a source of knowledge; preference for rational, cognitive, verbal, analytic

the pole of communitas to the women's movement, with its characteristics perceived as female. "We" represent the creative and transformative characteristics of ecstatic communitas, while "they" stand for stratification, status, and social structure. The out-of-structure quality of the experience of communitas is used to describe the position of a group. A number of women's liberation themes can be recognized among the attributes of communitas: an emphasis on personal experience; a repudiation of role playing and status markers; women's liberation demeanor; a criticism of monogamy and the nuclear family; a belief in radical egalitarianism; and an assumption of moral superiority associated with structural inferiority.

Let me note here that many aspects of feminist "analysis" are clarified if one understands the implicit assumption that women represent communitas while men represent power and hierarchy. For example, feminists frequently discuss the relationship between women and male physicians with an intensity and fury that can be difficult for an outsider to understand. In addition to concrete complaints—that male psychiatrists "brainwash" women to accept a Freudian view of themselves as incomplete beings who need marriage and children to fulfill themselves; that medical care is unfeeling, perfunctory, and patronizing; that gynecologists are often men with little sympathy for female feelings and problems—an important *symbolic* element is involved. If men represent hierarchy, then physicians are close to the top of the ranking. The feminist image, then, of the well-dressed gynecologist standing near a supine woman, whose feet are imprisoned in stirrups and whose sexual organs are exposed, is the symbol par excellence of the relationship between the hierarchical, powerful male and the exposed, powerless female.

One reason that communitas is attributed to women is that in the feminist movement "we" are female and "they" are male. This perception of communitas as the property of a specific group is reinforced by the ambiguous and inferior position of women within the social structure. De Beauvoir expresses this ambiguous lack of differentiation in philosophic form:

... the relation of the two sexes is not quite like that of two electrical poles, for man represents both the positive and the neutral, as is indicated by the common use of *man* to designate human beings in general; whereas woman represents only the negative, defined by limiting criteria, without reciprocity. . . . She is defined and differentiated with reference to man and not he with reference to her; she is the incidental, the inessential as opposed to the essential. He is the Subject, he is the Absolute—she is the Other.[18]

Hacker, on the other hand, uses a sociological framework to apply the concept of marginality to the position of women.[19] Turner, citing Douglas' view that "what is unclear and contradictory, from the perspective of social definition, tends to be regarded as ritually unclean," notes that ambiguous and marginal personae are generally regarded as polluting to those who have not been "inoculated" against them.[20] Hoffman supports this view of women as marginal (and polluting): in Greece, where women are on the margins of the social structure, acting as intermediaries to link groups through marriage, they are considered impure and wicked—until the death of their husbands, when their structural position alters and they are no longer regarded as polluting.[21] Middle-class women in American society also occupy a less differentiated position than men: female social status derives primarily from fathers or husbands, and can alter radically after marriage or divorce.[22] Female status reflects that of males; it has little independent existence.

The belief of feminists that women represent communitas, and the structurally ambiguous undifferentiated position of women, reinforce one another. In addition, many characteristics traditionally ascribed to women in our society resemble the attributes of communitas. Bakan, for example, associates the female personality with "communion," characterized by contact, openness, union, and the sense of being at one with other organisms, while the male personality is seen as preoccupied with agency, manifested in self-protection, self-assertion, self-expansion, and the urge to master." [23] Again, moral superiority joined with structural inferiority has been attributed to females since the 1830s, when intellectually and socially limited middle-class females were cast as the "moral" guardians of structurally superior males.[24] As a result, women suffragists in the 1890s asserted that women should be given the vote because they were more moral, more temperate, and more law-abiding than men.[25] In the same way coercion and power have been traditionally considered masculine traits,[26] in contrast to women's capacities for love and service and to their peaceful propensities; women's suffragists used similar arguments about society's need for these "female" charac-teristics at the turn of the century.[27] On occasion one will hear contemporary feminists use similar arguments to sup-port the need for more female legislators. Again, women are traditionally considered more personal and men more ab-stract; at the same time women are seen as intuitive, men as rational. Whether or not these characteristics are believed to be biologically or culturally determined, whether or not they can actually be found in more women than men, these attributes are part of the traditional female role in our society.

Thus, three mutually reinforcing factors influence the feminist perception of communitas as a female characteristic: (1) the association of communitas with a particular group or social movement by its adherents, (2) the ambiguous and marginal position of women within the social structure, and (3) the similarity between the attributes of communitas and characteristics traditionally ascribed to women in our society.

I have said that communitas refers to an experience. But this brief, ecstatic experience can be extended and used as a guide for behavior. In addition, the attributes of communitas can be used to outline a joyful new society where commu-nitas will become a way of life.

Turner distinguishes three forms of communitas:

1. *Existential* or *spontaneous* communitas—approx-imately what the hippies today would call "a happen-

ing" and William Blake might have called "the winged moment as it flies" or, later, "mutual forgiveness of each vice."

2. *Normative* communitas, where, under the influence of time, the need to mobilize and organize resources, and the necessity for social control among the members of the group in pursuance of these goals, the existential communitas is organized into a perduring social system.

3. *Ideological* communitas, which is a label one can apply to a variety of utopian models of societies based on existential communitas.

Turner notes that

> ideological communitas is at once *an attempt to describe the external and visible effects—the outward form, it might be said—of an inward experience of existential communitas,* and to spell out the optimal social conditions under which such experiences might be expected to flourish and multiply.[28]

The attempt to extend the experience of communitas to form the basis of rules for behavior and a plan for a new society is characteristic of women's liberation as opposed to women's rights groups. The belief that communitas is the property of a particular group, in this case women, links the experience of communitas undergone by that group to the rules for behavior. The group experiences and is energized by communitas: feminists feel a sense of ecstatic community, of merging, of "we-ness." The group then perceives itself as characterized by the attributes of communitas: *we* are more egalitarian, less hierarchical, less powerful and oppressive, more supportive. These attributes become norms or oughts— we *should* be this way, and when we behave differently we are being "like them." This is accompanied by the search for a revolutionary new society, where full-time permanent communitas will be present and its opposite pole of social structure, status system, and organization will be abolished.

Is such institutionalized communitas "really" communitas? Turner notes that the extension of communitas is within the domain of structure and observes that in religious movements, when leaders' charisma is "routinized," the communitas of followers is also routinized or institutionalized.[29] Clearly, institutionalized communitas and routinized charisma differ from the original, ecstatic, interpersonal experiences. They are, however, clearly related to, and based upon, them. Perhaps it is less important to decide what these institutionalized or routinized phenomena should be called than to observe and discuss their characteristics. Among these characteristics is the fact that what we might call "primary" charisma and communitas cannot be observed; they can only be experienced. An outside observer will not see communitas or charisma, only its effect upon participants. In addition, people rarely know that they have experienced communitas or charisma: the experience is perceived as a function of the group, the belief, the charismatic leader. It is the outside observer who names and categorizes these phenomena. Institutionalized communitas and routinized charisma, on the other hand, are more easily perceived by participants and observers: they consist of a set of rules and a utopian blueprint that can be discussed, followed, violated. The primary phenomena, then, are ecstatic and essentially indescribable, except perhaps by poetry. The institutionalized phenomena are within the realm of discourse; although they, too, cannot be seen or touched, they can be communicated, disputed, codified, and changed.

Although it is much discussed in women's liberation circles, the concept of communitas is not formulated as such. Instead, communitas is discussed in terms of its opposites; these are called "elitism" and "oppression."

I have described the principle of radical egalitarianism in the university action group that I observed. Radical egalitarianism is a women's liberation premise and goal: it is both assumed and sought. Radical egalitarianism is based on a belief that everyone has equal potential, and it includes rules of behavior to encourage the realization of this potential. Rules to abolish inequity and hierarchy lead quite naturally to women's liberation organizational principles, banning fixed leadership roles and group structure. When communitas is extended into rules for behavior, then, it leads to principles of organization designed to eliminate hierarchy in human relationships, and in feminist relationships in particular. The violation of these rules is called "elitism," which is perceived to be the opposite of feminism (or communitas).

A naive observer of women's liberation groups might find the frequent use of the word "elitism" bewildering—it is used in dissimilar contexts and appears to refer to very different phenomena. When elitism is conceptualized as the *opposite of communitas*, however, its meaning and use are clarified. The term has an essential ambiguity, which stems in part from its relation to one pole of a set of oppositions: elitism is the figure always perceived against the implicit ground of communitas.[30] Behavior related to social structure, hierarchy, and status system is elitist. The opposite pole, of communitas, nondifferentiation, and radical egalitarianism, has no name—it is "feminist" or "the way women do it."

Because communitas is always conceived in contrast to its opposite half, it can be difficult to perceive. Behavioral communitas is a set of normative expectations; one cannot "see" the rules but only their violation: where elitism is, communitas is not.

Freeman discusses the "incorrect" use of elitism in women's liberation and points out that an individual cannot be elitist because the term refers to groups.[31] If one understands that the term is always used in women's liberation circles in contrast to the attributes of communitas, however, then an individual's bearing or behavior can, indeed, violate rules for behavior based on communitas.

A college student active in women's liberation told me she had finally figured out her roommate after ten years of friendship. She said: "Mia won't do the readings the rest of us had to do. She went to the teacher and got her own private reading list. And our whole group feels you shouldn't shave your legs, but Mia shaves her legs because it feels good. She just can't get together with a group of other women. I think of it as kind of a private elitism."

It is difficult to explain this student's use of the term elitism unless we contrast elitism with the merging and feeling-together of communitas. Mia did not violate communitas as radical egalitarianism but as communion: she cannot become a "we" with other women.

A college instructor planned a conference of feminist scholars. The idea was met with hostility, and she was asked whether she wanted a feminist conference or an academic conference. She asked why a conference could not be both. To the instructor's women's liberation friends, an academic feminist conference was a contradiction in terms because academic is essentially hierarchical and "feminist" is egalitarian.

I have discussed communitas as an ecstatic experience, and shown how it can be extended into a set of rules for behavior. Communitas is further extended into a utopian goal, a blueprint for a new society. In this new and liberated world, sexual inequality will be abolished; so will the economic, social, and racial class systems based upon it. *The opposite pole of communitas as a pattern for a new society is "oppression"*—the oppression experienced by subjugated groups today. The term oppression refers to social arrangements, where one group imposes an inferior position within the social structure upon another.

The difference between "elitism" and "oppression," then, when they are opposed to communitas, is both qualitative and quantitative. Elitism occurs between those in similar positions within the social structure: it is in opposition to communitas as a rule for behavior. Oppression occurs between those in structurally unequal positions: it is the opposite of communitas as a pattern for a new society.

Despite the fact that the radical egalitarianism of the new liberated feminist society to come is discussed in comparatively rational, political terms, it contains an apocalyptic element, an intimation of future joy, ecstasy, and communion that transcends a mere absence of hierarchy. One finds an implication that when radical egalitarianism is achieved in the new society, communitas will be a "full-time and exclusive way of life." [32] Thus, although described in instrumental, political terms, radical egalitarianism has a mystical, ecstatic, transformative aspect. It is, in short, an attribute of communitas.

Radical egalitarianism is a significant women's liberation assumption, behavioral rule, and goal. For example, the following is a quote from a feminist manifesto:

> The first principle of *The Feminists* is the principle of equality. Equality among *all* human beings is, for us, both a premise and a goal. The assumption underlying the existence of our group is that in political affairs all people have the right to contribute equally, and further, that everyone has the potential to do so. Politics in its broadest sense refers to interaction among people with respect to their shared world or life, rather than activities which are solitary or affect only a group of intimates. . . . Political abilities are general human abilities and we claim that potential in these areas is about the same in all people. We cannot prove this assumption but neither can the opposite (that inequalities are natural) be proven until we rid ourselves of all oppression, i.e., of any and all instances of unequal treatment or opportunity which create artificial inequalities among us. [33]

What I have called radical egalitarianism is called "equality" in women's liberation circles, which may confuse the concept with the equality sought by women's rights groups. If we examine the differences between the radical egalitarianism of women's liberation and the women's rights concept of equality we can illuminate the distinction between value-oriented and norm-oriented groups.

When asked to define a feminist, a member of my university action group wrote: "Someone committed to the destruction of sex roles and by extension to the destruction of hierarchy in every human relationship." This definition is related to the concept of radical egalitarianism, with the destruction of hierarchy going beyond equality of rights to an attempt to erase individual differences, which are seen as a kind of inequity or hierarchy. A similar attempt to abolish all differentiation was described during the early days of the Israeli kibbutz, where an archetypical example of radical egalitarianism is evident in a rule that all babies receive exactly the same amount of breast milk, since they should all weigh the same number of kilos. Says Spiro of this: "Individual differences among infants were not recognized." [34] Although this concept was called *shevayon*, or "equality," in the kibbutz,[35] it was closer to *identity*: rather than take into account an infant's size, needs, and nature, the early pioneers attempted to force each infant to consume the same amount of food. The word, "equality," was the same, but the concept was clearly far more encompassing than that of equal rights.

Interestingly, in the kibbutz this concept of *shevayon*, or radical egalitarianism, was associated with a reaction against formal structure, against rank and prestige distinctions, with a radical repudiation of all differences between the sexes, and an antileadership ethic so strong that calling an individual a leader or manager was considered an insult.[36] We find here a set of interconnected beliefs or values, which are related to what Diamond calls "the utopian process." [37] This set of interconnected values can be called a utopian paradigm, with behavioral rules designed to transform individuals, relationships, and, ultimately, society. A large number of such rules consists of prohibitions, since what *is*, is to be abolished or transformed into its opposite.

In contrast to the definition of feminism as a destruction of hierarchy, another member of the university action group defined a feminist as "someone who believes in equal opportunities and equal responsibilities in all aspects of life for women and men." Here is a more traditional definition of equality, with no attempt to abolish differentiation to achieve identity. In this definition it is not hierarchy (including individual differences) but *discrimination* that is to be banned. Here we see the norm-oriented attempt to extend the norm of equality to another group, in this case women. Such a definition of equality is easier to implement; adherents are not required to subordinate their abilities to a somewhat mystical concept of the group; self-development is not perceived as competing with the development of others. The aim here is to remove outside forces that impede self-development.

We can see, then, how a value-oriented group tries to redefine basic conceptions. Despite the fact that a term such as "equality" has a rational, political connotation, the women's liberation definition has an almost mystical element, linked to the utopian dream of totally transforming individuals and society.

STRUCTURE AND SYMBOLISM

There is a temptation with a fixed typology of social movements to force observed phenomena into an ideal conceptual or geographical category, which obscures relationships between parts of a movement. When fixed typologies are abandoned in favor of a processual multigroup model, various conceptual schemata can be applied to groupings *within* social movements. For example, although Wallace's description of revitalization movements is processual and is, in fact, cited by Smelser in his description of value-oriented beliefs, Wallace does not consider the relationship between "revitalization" and "reform" elements in a single social movement.[38] This may be related to an implicit model of a single bureaucratic structure at the center of a movement:

As the group of converts expands, it differentiates into two parts: a set of disciples and a set of mass followers. The disciples increasingly become the executive organization, responsible for administering the evangelistic program, protecting the formulator, combating heresy, and so on. As the executive part of the movement, the disciples also increasingly become full-time specialists in the work of the movement. In this they are economically supported by the mass followers, who continue to play their roles in the existing culture, devoting part of their time and money to the movement. The tricornered relationship between the formulators, the disciples and the mass followers is given an authoritarian structure—even without the formalities of older or bureaucratic organizations—by the charismatic quality of the formulator's image.[39]

With the multigroup model, bureaucratic and egalitarian phenomena can exist side by side in a single social movement.[40] Examination and analysis of such "mixed" movements are facilitated when an a priori structure is not assumed before investigation. Distinctions between "magical" as opposed to "rational" means, between "nonrealistic" and "realistic" conflict, between "class" and "status" issues, between a search for total as opposed to partial, and personal as opposed to social change, or value-oriented vs. norm-oriented movements can be used to explore differences between groups within a single social movement.[41] Many of these distinctions are clearly related, being based on a differentiation between utopian movements (or groups) whose goals appear to an outsider to be relatively impractical or "expressive," and more pragmatic movements (or groups) with comparatively "realistic" goals.

Once we concede that a movement can be "mixed," and in fact frequently is, we can explore the relationship between different types of groups, examining what each type contributes to the movement. (This frees the observer from the necessity of perceiving a "lunatic fringe" of unruly followers who do not understand or obey the central leader's plans and goals.) We are then able to perceive the distinctive contribution to the women's movement made by utopian women's liberation groupings.

My case study of a woman's liberation action group explored a series of contradictions between observed behavior and what the women said, and appeared to believe, they were doing. Feminist operating principles, which I observed being violated more often than they were followed, were based on a series of traits which were frequently attributed to women, as opposed to "the way men do things." Radical egalitarianism was opposed to hierarchy; self-actualization to repression; sisterhood and cooperation to exclusion and coercion; and, personal experience to sterile abstraction. If these female (or feminist) attributes are interpreted as a literal description of a difference between the sexes, logical difficulties follow. For one thing, feminists assert that no difference between men and women has been proved and that apparent differences can be explained by different child-rearing practices for boys and girls and by inequality of opportunity. A contradiction takes place when feminists state that women are more peaceful, communal, and egalitarian at the same time that they declare no inherent difference between the sexes. The contradiction is on occasion recognized, with explanations that sex-related socialization practices emphasize certain characteristics in males and others in females, and that the "male" characteristics are becoming dangerous in today's world.[42] The descriptions of the disvalued "masculine" attributes are, however, more frequent than their attribution to upbringing, and the traits are most often discussed as though they were in some way quintessentially male. Thus feminists talk of "masculine structure" and "male types of groupings," with an implication that these formalized and hierarchical methods of organization are the natural way men do things, as opposed to the less structured, more peaceful, communal women's way.[43] When conflict, hierarchy, and the search for power among feminists are discussed by other feminists, the offenders are frequently described as being "like men."

Logical difficulties with this differentiation between the sexes vanish when it is viewed as a symbolic opposition. In this case the existence of the symbolism, and the function it serves, are significant whether or not the description corresponds with actual traits and behaviors. Because the women's movement lacks formal, bureaucratic structure and central leaders, this basic symbolic differentiation between the "women's way" and "the way men do things" plays a vital role—unifying and organizing the entire movement.

This symbolism originated in women's liberation groupings. Despite the fact that women's rights organizations are less bound by rules based on this symbolic opposition, the attributes of sisterhood also provide self-definition for these more pragmatically oriented groups. Carden discusses members' determination to run NOW "according to certain idealistic principles characteristic of the feminist movement in general, rather than according to the impersonal fashion of the male establishment." Among these "idealistic" principles are antielitism, antiauthoritarianism, a consensus model of decision making ("in contrast to the adversary model of the 'male world' "), and a belief that a leader can be legitimately sanctioned for forcing her ideas on the group.[44]

Women's liberation, then, provides the entire women's movement with an ideological and symbolic focus. The vision of sisterhood energizes and unites women. The concept of "the women's way" offers an emblem of the nature of women, the way they behave (or should behave), and a dream of a new joyful and liberated society where everyone will be like this. The symbolic attributes provide a group identity, a boundary differentiating "us" from "them," women from men, feminists from nonfeminists.

The utopian attempt to institutionalize sisterhood and the women's way and base a society upon their characteristics must inevitably fail, however. One cannot maintain a structureless structure, a self-actualizing nondifferentiation, a powerless revolution. It is an impossible task, but an inspiring one.

In discussing means and ends of both branches of the women's movement, I said that women's rights groups sought reformist goals by gradualist means, while women's liberation groups had revolutionary goals. The means used by women's liberation groups were not discussed. Although verbally violent, women's liberation means tend to be somewhat ambiguous because of the built-in contradiction between the symbolism of the women's way and instrumental activity.

Women's rights groups, then, whose members are inspired by the ideology of sisterhood without being limited by the necessity of following its principles, tend to be result-oriented ("like men"). Groups operate to achieve concrete social changes: sex-discrimination charges are filed against a state university; a lawsuit is instituted to bar public funds and facilities to the Little League because they do not allow girls to join; kits are prepared, with articles and arguments for feminists to use against foes of the Equal Rights Amendment; staff women file formal charges of sex discrimination against two national newsmagazines.[45]

Women's liberation groups, on the other hand, work to "change women's heads." Speakouts are held on Rape and Motherhood; an underground radical newspaper is "taken over" by a feminist coup; two hundred women stage an eleven-hour sit-in at a women's magazine to protest the image of women and their status at the magazine.[46] It is difficult for women's liberation groups to work for concrete social changes; concrete action takes organization, and long-range organization is arduous for a group that prefers to think of itself as leaderless and structureless. In addition, a group must utilize the existing power structure in order to work for specific changes: lawsuits must be instituted, promotions for women sought, and powerful individuals mobilized. One must work within the structure to alter that structure or create a revolution—which is difficult without leadership and organization. Thus, women's liberation groups tend to take short-range actions, raise consciousnesses, formulate theory— and talk revolution.

Carden quotes a NOW member as saying: " 'NOW is getting something done' but is 'treating the symptoms more than the causes [whereas] Women's Liberation is getting little done' but is 'going to the root causes.' " In a similar vein, a member of the New York Radical Feminists wrote: "For quite some time now I've been developing a new respect for what we've always called the reformists. They want specific ameliorative changes in women's lives; we want changed heads." [47]

In summary, value- and norm-oriented groups fulfill different functions in the women's movement. The utopian value-oriented groupings provide an ideology, a symbolic strategy to express and articulate the distinctiveness of the movement; norm-oriented organizations work for specific changes in the status of the collectivity. Both are necessary. A group must be created where none was perceived, and that group must be organized to improve its status.

11
Change and the Women's
Movement: The Ripple Effect

Contradictory accounts of the state and accomplishments of the women's movement are constantly being published. While some commentators write as though the movement is finished, falling away from its original goals and achievements, others discuss the growth and accomplishments of the movement as though it were accelerating.[1]

When the movement is divided into two main branches with different values, means, and goals, it becomes apparent that both accounts may be true. Many women's liberation groups have fragmented, discontinued, become encapsulated, or adopted more instrumental operating procedures and more concrete gradualist goals. At the same time, women's rights groups have grown; feminism is spreading to new places; and the status of women within the system is being improved.

Like the ripples from a pebble tossed into water, feminism has expanded in widening ripples of change: personally, from feminist groups to women's lives; in organizations, from the utopian center to the reformist periphery; through social classes, from middle- to lower- and working-class groups; and geographically, from large urban centers to smaller cities and suburban communities. As the outer ripples have spread, however, the center has dissolved.

A CHANGED LIFE

Many examinations of attempts to achieve change focus on the rhetoric and disappointments, with little attention paid to activities that may effect small but cumulative changes in people's lives. Hence, it may be illuminating to see the change in the life of one woman, whose feminist career is presented in the Appendix in more detail.

In 1969 Sarah Miller was living in a cold-water walk-up apartment in New York City, feeling lonely and abandoned. She had little money; it was difficult to go out with two babies; and her husband was rarely home. She attended a discussion group on child care composed of young mothers, which was affiliated with a New Left organization. Almost every woman who took part in that group later organized a cooperative children's play group. Sarah herself started two play groups, one for each child. She reported that in her two child-care groups, only two women considered themselves feminists at first, while more than twenty so defined themselves by the time the groups disbanded. Each woman who attended the 1969 child-care discussion group seems to have learned two things: (1) there were others who felt as isolated as she, and (2) something could be done to change her situation. In forming a play group she acquired organizing skills, friends in the same situation, time for herself, and confidence in her own ability to change her life.

Let us consider this process. The original discussion group and the child-care groups that sprang from it were political phenomena; they influenced women to take steps to change their lives and in the process changed their perceptions of reality—raised their consciousness. These changes were both personal and social, and they started in groups—child care, consciousness raising, and feminist action groups. The effects of change, joined to an awareness of shared problems as women, helped forge a constituency of active women dedicated to further change as they worked to alter self-images and life situations.

Sarah, who thought of herself as a bookish person with little ability to get along with people, discovered she enjoyed speaking in public and working with large groups. Not only her self-image but also her life situation improved. Her marriage became more stable. She moved to a more communal situation where she was able to share child-care and housekeeping responsibilities while still perceiving herself, her husband, and her children as an individual family. She discovered and prepared herself for work she found interesting, in the women's health field, and toward which she had a deep feminist commitment. From the groups where feminist activity had started, feminism spread to her life. When Sarah was interviewed in May 1973, it was impossible to categorize the majority of her activities as personal or political; they were both. Sarah's life had become part of the political field; the field had become part of her life.

Nevertheless, when interviewed Sarah expressed guilt because school, the commune, child care, and job-hunting left little time for activity in feminist groups. When I suggested that the movement had become part of her life rather than her having to go out to the movement, and perhaps that was one of the things the women's movement was about, she agreed, looking surprised. She appears to have thought of involvement in terms of formal feminist groups and felt that her feminist activity had diminished.[2]

In the same way, although she mentioned her cooperative play groups and the commune as feminist or feminist-inspired groups, she did this on second thought, as though discovering the connection as she spoke. These appear to have been perceived as part of her personal life, not her political activity. Sarah agreed that participation in the women's movement had changed her life, but it is not clear that she had previously seen her life as so changed.

The relationship between personal change and the women's movement, then, may not be apparent to the women whose lives have changed as a consequence of feminist activity. Such women seem to perceive most clearly that the amount of time spent with formal feminist groups has been curtailed. Some may then conclude that the movement is losing momentum and that feminists, including themselves, are retreating into their personal lives. An outside observer might disagree with this conclusion. Despite the fact that the original impetus, the formal group activity, may have subsided, the altered life styles, self-images, and career patterns stimulated by the women's movement may continue to spread widening ripples of change.

THE GROUP AS A WAY OF LIFE

Contrasted to this ripple effect, which moves outward from group activity to an altered life, is another and contradictory process whereby women move closer into the feminist group. Rather than transforming the personal into political, some women attempt to make the political personal—they want the group to become their personal lives.

Sarah described a series of conflicts in an abortion action group that illuminates this attempt to expand the functions of a feminist group so that it becomes an individual's personal life. After the liberalized New York State abortion law went into effect, some members of a feminist abortion group wished to move into political action, while others did not. Sarah discussed the difference between the two factions, those who wished to move into political activism and left when the group did not do so, and those who wished to continue abortion referral.

"The people who split off then, which I did ... whether it was a class thing or education. . . . I never had a shit job in my life! But some of the women loved working on abortion referral; it was much more interesting and satisfying than the low-level shit jobs they had held. . . . The sort of people who did the work were the sort who had jobs they hated—many quit and lived on their savings and unemployment."

Sarah called this a "class difference." Although she was a housewife, with two young children and little money, Sarah had a Ph.D., which gave her access to comparatively well-paid, high-status work when and if she wished. She described a later conflict in the same group, between women who still wanted to continue abortion referral, who wished the group to become an "alternative service" outside the medical establishment, and those who wanted to pressure the existing medical establishment to be more responsive to women's needs.

> "The people who wanted an alternative service were those who felt they couldn't exist within the system. It was that class thing again. People who could see work outside the project as meaningful, who could get interesting jobs, who were more educated, higher class, more interested in political organization, didn't feel the need for an alternative system. Those interested in service couldn't really get meaningful jobs outside. In the project they were running their own show; it was stimulating, exciting work to them. . . . *There were many women who had decided not to marry—they needed the group, they needed the support and warmth that the group offered—it was a way to define their lives."*

The women with fewest alternatives in the outside world wished to turn their feminist group into a way of life. Rather than attempting to change institutions within the larger society, which meant entering that society and engaging with it, the group was to be an "alternative."

Part 1 of this book discussed the increasing segregation from nonbelievers of committed revolutionary feminists, showing how this segregation might culminate in a bridge-burning act where, by becoming a lesbian, a woman could sever ties with the outside world. Women such as these, with few connections to the outside world, want the most from their feminist groups. If we reexamine the split in a feminist theater group mentioned in chapter 8, which was variously reported as a split between lesbian and heterosexual women, or between those who wanted the group to be primarily a way of life and those who wanted a performing group, it becomes apparent that the factors may be related. The most committed and segregated feminists are the ones who need their groups to fill emotional as well as instrumental functions; the group must be a family, a haven, a way of life, a mechanism for earning a living.[3] The feminist group, in short, must replace the traditional role of husband and nuclear family. Rather than helping to change a participant's outside life, the group is to *become* that life.

Let us reconsider the proliferation of meetings described in the case study on a women's liberation action group (see pp. 136-39). The meetings served to unite the women who attended them, with their frequency helping to drive out those individuals with outside interests and commitments. The number of meetings was connected with a difficulty in making decisions and an emphasis upon a consensus model of decision making. There was probably another factor influencing the number of meetings: the need on the part of some members for the group as a way of life. Meetings were held evenings and weekends—the time when those with other emotional commitments might be busy, the time when those who lacked such commitments might need a feeling of closeness and belonging. The group as a way of life, however, can conflict with the group as instrumental entity. The proliferation of meetings can select against women who lack both time and emotional need for a primary interactive group—women simply interested in working for social change. The emphasis upon nondifferentiation, which might indeed promote closeness and a sense of communion, can also suppress or force out individuals with the leadership abilities necessary to carry out social-change projects. For example, as the participants with outside options gradually withdrew from the abortion group described by Sarah Miller, those who needed the group as a way of life continued to do abortion referral. But the service these women provided was criticized by a feminist review group, which concluded that the price was high and service to women insufficient. Providing abortions had become by that time a somewhat secondary purpose: abortions were legal; there were competing abortion-referral services; and the group as a way of life had overshadowed its instrumental functions. Such a group then becomes encapsulated, with little interaction with and effect upon the outside world. The group as a way of life seems difficult to sustain for any period of time, and some feminists have expressed disappointment and disillusion with the women's movement when it could not meet their interpersonal needs.

THE RIPPLE EFFECT IN ORGANIZATIONS

Perhaps one reason the movement has been unable to meet the personal needs of revolutionary feminists who have burned their bridges and want the movement to provide an emotional focus for their lives is that an organizational ripple effect can be observed, similar to the widening circles of individual change. Thus the early, influential revolutionary women's liberation groups are dissolving at the same time that the movement spreads in widening circles, reaching a new constituency. By 1973 many early women's liberation groups that created and defined women's liberation theory, analysis, and tactics had dissolved or appeared to be losing focus and direction. The Feminists, which split off from NOW in 1968 when Ti-Grace Atkinson disagreed with the hierarchical structure and reformist goals of NOW, had become an extremely small, highly disciplined group that was considered rigid by many feminists.[4] The New York Radical Women, organized in 1968, had dissolved, as had WITCH and Redstockings, both of which had started as factions within Radical Women. And Columbia Women's Liberation, founded by Kate Millett among others in 1968, was dormant and did not reconstitute the following year. A number of dedicated feminists active in women's liberation since the mid-1960s expressed discouragement about the movement. One woman said she thought women were deserting the movement because it could not give them what they needed and they were turning to men for security, support, a future. Another said of herself and her former women's liberation associates: "Everyone's escaping into hedonism. Or masochism. Or both." [5]

But as these utopian theoretical groups began to falter, new result-oriented units sprang up. When Columbia Women's Liberation stopped meeting in the spring of 1973, many of its most active participants started working with a new group toward a single, extremely pragmatic goal—to unionize the university's secretarial and clerical workers, most of whom were female.

Women's caucuses in professional groups, and women's professional groups, have proliferated.[6] Student women's liberation groups frequently disapproved of "joining the system." The system instead was to be transformed. But members of such groups have now graduated. Like it or not, they are part of the system, and many are now working with professional groups to improve that system. The professional organizations work on specific projects to advance the status of women: research projects, lobbying efforts, class-action suits. Rather than formulating revolutionary theory, these political pressure groups undertake sophisticated and well-planned actions to advance the interests of their members.

Not all women's liberation groups have dissolved in the widening ripples of change. Some have altered structure and tactics. Instead of repudiating leadership and formal organization (as being "like men"), they have adopted more bureaucratic structures, switched to voting instead of consensus decision making, and hired staff workers to do the routine work. Instead of denigrating power as a masculine trait, these groups have begun to work for power for women.

As the radical center of women's liberation changed tactics or dissolved, the periphery has expanded and becomes energized. Nonfeminist groups experienced a feminist surge. An informant described how a member of Chicago NOW was invited to talk to New York City Girl Scout leaders in 1972:

> There they were, all those women, and some of them were really *old!* They were sitting there in their beauty-parlor hairstyles, wearing Girl Scout hats and ties. And if you had told them someone was going to talk to them about women's liberation, they would probably have walked out. But they thought she was going to talk about what it was like growing up as a girl. And then she started to tell them about growing up, and how there were some things you were told you couldn't do even if you wanted to, and some avenues were closed to you, and how boys could choose what they wanted to be and do, but girls had limited choices and career options. And how as you got older, things just got worse, and talented women did volunteer work while men used the same ability to get ahead in their fields. And those women sat there and listened and some of them even began to cry. And they said, "Yes, it's true! That's the way it is." And they decided it was time for the Girl Scouts to get involved in feminism, and they hired the woman from NOW to be in charge of the new program.

The Young Lords, a revolutionary mixed-sex Puerto Rican organization, was another group influenced by feminism. An informant reported that the Young Lords had a women's caucus and that they had initiated men's consciousness-raising sessions to discuss *machismo* with a view to eradicating it. Groups such as the YWCA, which had been founded by feminists but had lost its feminist impetus over the years, and the National Council of Jewish Women also became involved in feminist issues.[7] At the same time, women were making tangible professional advances. Law school became popular among women, and feminist law firms have been opening. In three years, the number of women enrolled in medical schools doubled—from 9.6 percent of total enrollment in 1970–71 to 15.4 percent in 1974–75.

Feminism has reached a group of women who were formerly peripheral to the primarily white middle-class women's movement. Black women, union women, and ethnic women have all formed their own groups. Airline stewardesses, once ranked with Playboy bunnies as prime female sex-and-service symbols, have become militant: two stewardess organizations are engaged in legal action and job protest for higher salaries, better working conditions, and a less demeaning image.

As revolutionary women's liberation groupings dissolved, more pragmatic women's rights organizations expanded. Membership in the National Organization for Women (NOW) has grown from about 1000 in 1967 to an estimated 60,000 in 1975, with a budget that went from $7000 in 1967 to more than $1 million for 1976. National NOW is presently split by a factional dispute, but local NOW chapters appear to be little affected, with 750 chapters growing in number, gaining in membership, and undertaking increasing projects to advance the position of women.[8]

Female-owned and feminist businesses have been multiplying. In 1976 a New York Association of Women Business Owners was formed to provide technical assistance, publicity, and influence legislation.

Feminist coalitions have been organizing at an accelerating rate. The New York Women's Lobby, formed in 1975, consists of organizations as diverse as the Coalition of Catholics for a Free Choice, Lesbian Feminist Liberation, the Progressive Household Technicians, the New York Civil Liberties Union, and Women's Equity Action League. The National Women's Agenda, organized in 1975, is composed of an even larger number of extremely diverse groups. Another group formed in 1975 is the National Coalition of Women and Girls in Education, consisting of a wide variety of groups interested in combating discrimination in education. Such coalitions focus less on revolution or theory than on specific actions to improve the status of women.

The ripple effect is geographic as well. Although commentators appear to disagree about where the movement is making the largest gains, the general consensus seems to be that it is spreading from major cosmopolitan cities into suburban areas and smaller cities.[9] The largest number of new local women's groups have been formed in communities where there was no previous feminist activity. Therefore, feminism is found in more areas today than in the late 1960s and early 1970s.[10]

In the summer of 1974, a counterculture newspaper in Bellingham, Washington, was edited by women. It was reminiscent of similar New York City publications of 1969 and 1970. The publication contained a lyrical piece on discovering lesbianism, an article comparing prostitution and low-level female jobs, articles on rape and on herbs, and an essay describing a short-lived but apparently satisfying attempt to run a communal feminist coffeehouse. The issue was suffused with a sense of energy, hope, and excitement, expressed in comments by the writers: "women working together ... such strength, such feelings, such sisterhood, a new type of consciousness, an energy flow that is so high and such fun, and I've discovered something inside me that is blossoming."[11] A feminist newspaper with similar format from New York City, for August 1974, had a more somber tone. One article discussed conflict in a lesbian organization, where fighting became so violent that the police were called; another told how one woman beat up another at a vegetarian feminist meeting; and a third announced a demonstration to protest a cut in eligibility for federal day care. The New York paper did have one thing the Bellingham paper lacked: advertisements by and a listing of sixty-one women's businesses—from carpentry to exterminating to typesetting.[12]

I have described the way in which the early women's liberation groupings dissolved or altered tactics and structure. These utopian groups dreamed of abolishing hierarchy, leadership, and structure.

Hierarchy, leadership, and structure are still with us. But women are reaching higher positions within the structure. The use of power has not been abolished, but some women are achieving power. Values have not been changed; but "feminist" values, while violated as rules of operating procedure, still function as symbolic strategy for defining an interest group.

The utopian women's liberation groupings provided impetus for these changes. Their dream of a transformed "women's world" helped recruit and mobilize women and gave the more pragmatic and reformist groups the momentum to achieve tangible changes in the position of women.

The women's movement, then, is becoming less value-oriented, with lesser impetus toward a total and revolutionary transformation of self and society. Instead, norm-oriented elements of the movement are growing. Goals have become more "concrete"; they are action goals involving advancement rather than moral goals based on a kind of spiritual transformation. Despite a backlash, change is occurring, but not the central moral transformation dreamed of by the utopian groups. Instead of destroying the system, women are beginning to get a piece of the action.

12

Some Questions
with Few Answers

How much change is "enough" change?

O'Neill, in a stimulating analysis of the nineteenth-century women's movement, examined the early branch of radical feminism, which called for "new institutions as well as new ways of thinking," and showed how this gave way to a more conservative and "altruistic" doctrine that helped win the vote for women. He believes that if women are to secure complete equality, today's feminists will again have to challenge the fundamental institutions of monogamy and the nuclear family. "In theory," he states, "women today are free to do as they please; in practice, their heavy obligations as wives and mothers prevent them from exercising the rights they nominally enjoy." [1]

In the final analysis, the traditional "domestic structure" of today's nuclear family is central to women's dilemma in our society. Women's liberation goes to the "root cause" of the problem and calls for a radical transformation of values, relationships, and institutions; women's rights groups attack symptoms, seeking palliative and redressive measures to raise the status of women.

What is the solution to the traditional domestic structure? Women's liberation theorists, who tend to be childless, call for drastic measures to remove women's "heavy obligations as wives and mothers": Firestone states that test-tube babies are the only way to free women from primary child-care responsibility; Millett suggests that children be reared by "trained practitioners" who have chosen child care as a vocation; and Greer proposes that a group of congenial people buy a farmhouse in southern Italy and have their children reared by the local peasants.[2] These suggestions have an air of cloud-cuckooland to an observer with children, especially if peasants' childrearing practices have been examined at close range, and in fact, one commentator compares the passages in feminist writings on children to *Playboy* magazine's treatment of women, finding in each the "same condescension and tendency to see the child [or woman] as an object rather than a person." [3]

Many feminists, in women's rights and women's liberation groups, seek government day care for children. But is day care a solution? (Who takes time off from work if the child gets the measles?) Or is it a palliative? Perhaps the real answer is a complete shift in sex roles so that men and women share equally the responsibility for children.

Can such a shift take place in more than a few isolated instances? Role sharing and role reversal have always been with us. But can role sharing become the cultural ideal and the statistical norm? Women's liberationists recognize that men will have to renounce a measure of ambition, a wish to move ahead in their fields, if they are to take time out to help care for children. This is quite consonant with an ideology that calls for a renunciation of power, hierarchy, and differentiation. Will fathers renounce a measure of self-actualization so that children can develop their fullest potential? Will mothers? Or will people renounce having children in favor of a utopia that lasts for just one generation?

Women's rights members, in advocating a higher position for women in the structure of power and control, appear to take it for granted that someone else will be taking care of the children of these powerful women. Who? Lower-class women with no access to power? To some extent the problem can be swept under the rug in a large organization such as NOW, where one task force seeks professional advancement for women, another calls for role sharing in child care (which would jeopardize professional advancement for both men and women), and still a third seeks advancement for poor and Third World women.

Perhaps Sarah Miller is closest to a solution that meets the needs of both mothers and children in our society. She lives in a communal situation where household chores and child rearing are shared, but privacy and the concept of individual families is retained. In 1974 Sarah noted that many of her feminist friends with children were moving into similar situations.

Can communes resolve the conflict between self-actualization for women and the needs of children? The Israeli kibbutz provides an equivocal answer.[4] Although abolished in the early days of the kibbutz, a division of labor based on sex seems to have returned. Children are communally reared, but women do most of the rearing and are concentrated in the housekeeping jobs, while men tend to specialize in the (more prestigious) farming and manual jobs.

Although he believes that feminists must challenge monogamy and the nuclear family if they are to achieve true equality, O'Neill does raise the possibility that the problem is essentially insoluble, that women's dilemma may be one of "the facts of life that simply have to be endured."[5] If the problem is insoluble, individual women may have to choose between professional advancement and having children, which is essentially today's situation. Such a choice is not a real answer, however. As Bailey points out, "Rules are internalized through the process of socialization, and they are kept in repair by various ritual devices and made immediate, almost tangible ... through symbolic objects."[6] If child rearing is primarily a female responsibility, women will be socialized—as indeed they are—so that this responsibility is internalized and sought. Only an exceptional and somewhat deviant woman will be able to break the cycle.

If, on the other hand, women are socialized to feel little or no responsibility for children, who will take the responsibility? The determining constraint may be population pressure: when the birthrate is perceived as too high, an ideology that rejects responsibility for childbearing, nurturance, and rearing becomes acceptable, even fashionable.[7]

Mead proposes that, in light of growing population pressures, only those women who regard childbearing and rearing as a vocation should have children, with young families living in a nonbiological extended family situation where children are able to interact with a variety of adults (and childless adults can interact with children). Those who lack this vocation would be encouraged to devote themselves to a wider sphere, rather than being socialized to believe that individual fulfillment is solely a function of marriage and family. In addition, older women whose children are grown would be encouraged to meet new challenges and take on new responsibilities.[8]

Women, in short, would choose between rearing children and another vocation; and men might make a similar choice.[9] If childbearing and child rearing are not highly rewarded, however, there is some danger that the individuals who "discover" they have a "vocation" for it will be precisely those with little interest or ability for anything else, possibly leading to a sort of negative natural selection.[10] On the other hand, if institutionalized child-care arrangements are available, so that gifted members of society can contribute to the gene pool while developing individual abilities, serious problems may arise over who is entitled to this double privilege.

It is worth noting here that many people may want both: self-actualization and children. The desire to have children may or may not be a product of socialization; we simply do not know enough at this time to be sure. If it is, how does one selectively socialize so that only a few individuals desire children? Intuitively, this does not appear to be the same sort of problem as how to make sure that only a few individuals want to be atomic physicists.

It is likely that, if people do want privileges, it is the women, as childbearers, rather than the men, who will be forced to choose between self-actualization and child rearing. Perhaps what Helene Deutsch calls a central conflict in a woman's life, between her role as an individual and that as "servant of the species," is essentially insoluble.[11]

If so, only palliative measures can help. In that case, the primary advantage of value-oriented approaches, such as that of women's liberation, is to act as a kind of reverse revolutionary karate, where escalated (and perhaps impossible) demands lead to tangible but moderate gains.

Appendix: Women's Movement Career of a Feminist Activist

The following outline is based upon interviews with one woman about her feminist career. Sarah Miller's experiences have been mentioned in the sections on becoming a feminist and change and the women's movement. Here is her entire story. She is not presented as "typical"; I was unable to identify a "typical" feminist. Her story is representative, however, illustrating feminist recruitment and activity. In addition, this account shows the feminist political field through time, illustrating the way in which groups begin, grow, shift, combine, change, split, and die.

Sarah Miller shares characteristics with many anthropological informants: she is unusually intelligent and reflective. She was such an articulate informant that I used her words throughout. Sarah was not selected in a random fashion (which would theoretically make her history more representative—or at least less statistically suspect). Instead, her name was volunteered when I was investigating an abortion project. After the first interview, it became clear that the abortion project was part of an ongoing process involving formation, fission, and fusion of a number of interrelated groups; it also became apparent that Sarah had reflected deeply on the events and groups with which she had been associated. I proposed the present project, of listing all the women's movement groupings with which Sarah had been involved. A second interview took place, which was tape-recorded. I organized my material and showed it to her at a third interview, where a number of details and dates were clarified. As I had promised, Sarah saw the completed material about her. She and I collaborated in altering identifying material, including her name and nationality.

The following was collected in response to a question: "Tell me about all the women's movement groups with which you were involved." As discussion proceeded, Sarah kept recalling more groups and expressed surprise at the number and variety of groups. She offered personal information spontaneously. This is listed in the left-hand column, with political activities on the right-hand side. At the beginning, Sarah's life situation influenced her movement involvement. Feedback came later, with movement ideas and activities affecting her personal life. After three years of women's movement involvement, Sarah's personal life and political activities began to merge. This material is placed in a central column, beginning on page 212. The account is arranged chronologically.

Personal	*Political*
1941: Sarah Sorenson Miller born in Stockholm, Sweden. Father, a professor of zoology; mother, a housewife who went to college when children were grown. Father's background, Swedish Protestant; mother's, Russian Jewish. Parents are former	

Personal	*Political*

communists, still politically leftist.

1962: Graduated from University of Stockholm. Married American journalist and political activist. Both came to United States. Entered Ph.D. program in cell biology at Columbia University on full scholarship.

1966: Received Ph.D. Became pregnant. Returned to Sweden with husband.

I never questioned that I would have children. I always wanted children very much. I came from a large family and saw children as an intrinsic part of life. One of the reasons I didn't see it as a contradiction in terms of the job was that coming from an upper-middle-class family on the one side, people had always had jobs and servants. I mean they had had a sort of independence, not only in terms of some income, but the sort of independence that comes with servants. For me that wasn't possible. I didn't really realize how much

Personal	*Political*

the contradiction between children and jobs comes out if you don't have money.

1967: First child born. Began to work full-time in a laboratory three months later.

I had my first child, and when he was three months old I went back to work full-time in Sweden with a feeling that . . . there was always this notion that I wanted to be independent, and a sort of [family] *history of independent educated women. So then I worked for thirteen months in Sweden, which was a big struggle, because not only did I want to spend more time with the child, but I found myself less and less interested in work.*

1968: Became pregnant with second child and stopped working four months later.

I was unable to really come out and say that I didn't want to do this sort of work, that my notions of a career were not . . . that I was not happy with

Personal	*Political*

*. . . I always wanted a
child but I used the fact
of pregnancy as a
perfectly respectable
social reason for stopping
work.*

1968: *Autumn*—Returned
to the United States.
December—Second child
born in New York City.

*Up until the time my
child was born I wanted
to get involved in
something but I didn't
really know what. Because
of my always having had
free health care and
feeling very strongly about
that, and because I was
using clinics—prenatal
clinics—I decided that was
an area I really wanted to
work in. Because . . . I was
living in an environment
where people were talking
about radicalism, and my
husband was a political
activist. And I knew I felt
emotionally about the
health issue deep enough
to be able to translate it
into . . . for it to underpin
a political consciousness.
What had come out of
my old left background
was a sense of distance*

between the words and all the stuff about working class and proletariat and all that—and who I was. There was no connection. I didn't feel any personal oppression, it was ideas. . . . I felt that in order for me to be able to do anything it was important to have sort of an emotional force and a sense of oppression. And to want to change something that I could feel was wrong in a personal way. And the health issue, having always had a free health system, was important in that way because I felt insulted every time the question of money came up.

1969: Lived in a sixth-floor walk-up tenement apartment with two young children and very little money. Husband rarely home.

    . . . my husband really didn't want to have anything to do with his family. He was not exactly thinking about leaving us, but he was having an affair with

*another women, which I
didn't know about at the
time. But he didn't want
to have another child; it
was me who wanted the
second child. He didn't
want to have anything to
do with the one he had.
He never did anything
around the house. He
never got up for the baby.
He was out all the time.
He was one hundred
percent involved in his
work. And I couldn't
count on him. So that I
felt personally very
oppressed in a way that I
never had before, totally
dependent on him
financially. And I had no
friends in New York. I
lived in a building with
several young children and
we all helped each other
out, and that was
incredibly important to
me. I could not possibly
have survived without
that. I came to depend on
neighbors—women—in a
very real way. So that
experience made me
identify with other
women, ordinary women,
in a way that, given my*

Personal	Political
background, a lot of things probably wouldn't have.	
January 1969	Attended discussion group on child care affiliated with Movement for a Democratic Society (New Left group). DURATION: Four months. TIME COMMITMENT: One meeting every two weeks. PERSONNEL: *One man got to know a lot of women at home with young babies and got the women together to talk.* CONSEQUENCES: *When we started talking, we all lived in all different parts of the city. But it made us realize that we didn't have to accept our isolated situation. And nearly all those women subsequently went into their neighborhoods, started a play group or worked in child care.*
Winter	Attended meetings of health group of Movement for a Democratic Society. DURATION: Very short period. TIME COMMITMENT: Sporadic attendance.

Personal	Political
	PERSONNEL: New Left men and women.
	CONSEQUENCES: Introduced Sarah to radical critique of American health system.
Spring 1969	Joined consciousness-raising group.
	DURATION: Four months.
	TIME COMMITMENT: One evening a week.
	PERSONNEL:

> *Most of the women were sort of "heavies" from SDS* [Students for a Democratic Society—New Left mixed-sex group]. *They weren't necessarily heavies but they came out of that experience. And I was the only one with children and I think I was the only one who was married.*

CONSEQUENCES:

> *It didn't work at all for me. Just made me very defensive. And that* [the consciousness-raising group] *fell apart. I didn't really talk about what I felt. There was no way in which people could relate to the problem I was facing with children: they could just sort of look on me and pity me, and pity wasn't what I wanted.*

Personal	*Political*
June 1969	Attended conference on Women's liberation at the New School.
	DURATION: Two days.
	PERSONNEL: 200 to 300 women attended.
	CONSEQUENCES:
	Everything that the women's movement was trying to say somehow came clear. And it affected me very deeply. And somehow around that time I got to know more women. And people started baby-sitting for me and taking care of the children—because of some notion of sisterhood. People started criticizing my husband because he wasn't participating at all. I also began to be able then to tell a few people how unhappy I was . . . and not feel it was my fault.
Summer	Organized a cooperative play group in her neighborhood and convinced the Parks Department to let the mothers use a building in the local playground for the group.
	DURATION: Two years.
	TIME COMMITMENT: One morning plus half a day on

Personal	*Political*

Political

administration/organization.
PERSONNEL: Neighborhood
mothers with children the
same age as Sarah's son.
CONSEQUENCES:

> *... it was very important
> to me in terms of this
> common feeling of
> working with women,
> respecting other ordinary
> women, feeling that you
> were struggling with the
> same thing.*

Attended discussion group
on women's health issues.
Group later named the
Women's Health Collective.
DURATION: One year.
TIME COMMITMENT: One
meeting a week, and outside
reading.
PERSONNEL:

> *A couple of women I
> knew at Health Pac* [a
> radical health
> organization] *decided to
> run a discussion group on
> health issues for women,
> and invited a number of
> women they knew who
> were interested.*

ACTIVITIES: Women taught
courses in women's health;
picketed a meeting of the
American College of
Obstetrics and Gynecology;
and prepared literature on

Personal	*Political*
	birth control, abortion, and the health system.
	CONSEQUENCES: Group was started as a summer workshop on health issues, to include consciousness raising on women and their bodies. A female lawyer attended one meeting and told the group she planned to prepare a lawsuit to permit abortion based on women's rights, if the women's movement would organize around the issue. The majority of group participants were interested. Those not interested in working on abortion remained as the Women's Health Collective. The others formed the Women's Abortion Project. Sarah participated in both groups.
Fall 1969	Helped organize the Women's Abortion Project. DURATION: Abortion project still existed in spring 1973, although name, personnel, and activities had changed, and Sarah was no longer with group. TIME COMMITMENT: Variable. On occasion, participants worked forty to fifty hours a week.

Personal	Political

PERSONNEL: Women interested in liberalizing or abolishing abortion laws.

There were two points of view, really: some people wanted to organize around the issue of abortion; some, around the women's movement.

ACTIVITIES:

It was really a kind of model of political organization: how things should be done. They wanted to find concrete things for people to do. Some people went to hospitals to get statistics about live births, number of abortions coming in. There were masses of petitions circulated; they were a device to talk to people on street corners and very effective. Some went to hospitals to ask for abortion facilities, to make them know that women were interested.

Sarah's phone number, along with the number of one other member, was on an early Women's Abortion Project leaflet. Women who wanted an abortion, which was then illegal, telephoned

her and came to her
apartment so she could give
them in person the names
and addresses of
abortionists. Participants
found plaintiffs for the
projected abortion lawsuit
who were willing to testify
about past abortions and a
possible need for future
abortions, and doctors to
testify about how they had
been unable to give advice
on necessary abortions. After
the liberalized New York
State abortion law went into
effect on July 1, 1970, the
project initiated a telephone
abortion-referral service.
Women from other states
were accompanied to
hospitals, with participants
claiming they were relatives,
to make them eligible for
New York abortions. When
saline abortions were
performed (on those more
than four months'
pregnant), participants took
out-of-state women to their
own homes and helped
deliver the fetus a few days
later.
CONSEQUENCES: Abortions
were procured for women
from all over the United

Personal	Political
	States. After the liberalized abortion law was passed, the abortion-referral service succeeded in lowering the price of abortions. Although the project generated much publicity, Sarah now believes that passage of the liberal New York State abortion law was influenced more by the efforts of groups such as NOW, which engaged in direct lobbying in Albany, than by the work of the abortion project.
December 1969	People to Abolish Abortion Laws formed. This was a coalition of abortion groups organized for a giant rally scheduled for March 28, 1970, which was, by chance, two days after the liberal New York State abortion law was passed. Sarah and other participants in the Women's Abortion Project spoke at meetings organized by this group. DURATION: Until March 28 rally. PERSONNEL: The coalition was organized by the Socialist Workers party, with male and female participants. ACTIVITIES: Meetings and demonstrations were

Personal	*Political*
	organized and the March 28 rally planned. There was some disagreement about means between the Socialist Worker organizers of the coalition and the participants in the Women's Abortion Project, who were dubious about the efficacy of rallies.
	CONSEQUENCES: Some of the women active in this group went on to form the Women's National Abortion Action Coalition (WONAAC) a year later, which also had ties with the Socialist Worker's party.
around Christmas 1969	Consciousness-raising group formed, which Sarah joined.
	DURATION: Seventeen months.
	TIME COMMITMENT: One evening a week.
	PERSONNEL: Ten women.

Most of these women had a history of work on the left . . . had come through the civil rights movement. They hadn't been among the women who initiated the women's movement on the left, but all of them had gone through something which made them understand how important it was to them.

Personal	Political
	There were always some people, I felt, who latched on to the women's movement because it seemed to be a growing thing, but this group of people—they had been active on the left and felt that the women's movement was personally and politically important.
	CONSEQUENCES:
	Emotional support . . . contact with women involved in a range of activities, which extended in experience when I was at home with the kids . . . friendship.
January 1970	Participated in attempt to form a radical city-wide coalition of women's groups to be called the Women's Union.
	DURATION: Three months.
	TIME COMMITMENT: Variable.
	PERSONNEL: Included members of Sarah's consciousness-raising group.
	ACTIVITIES: A manifesto was written:
	Our stance was sort of low-keyed: "Struggle where you work." We hoped that you would have groups of women

Personal	*Political*
	who taught in college, teachers' groups; a health group; a group who worked on child care; plus consciousness-raising groups that subscribed to this political view.... We had a few large meetings which were very well attended, and people were anxious to have an organization, but ...
	CONSEQUENCES:
	... although a lot of people came and I still think it could have worked if we had been different people, or whatever—it came to nothing.
Spring 1970	Organized a second cooperative play group for her younger child.
	DURATION: Almost two and a half years. Sarah left when her family moved to a different neighborhood.
	TIME COMMITMENT: One to two mornings a week.
	PERSONNEL: Primarily white middle-class neighborhood mothers, although some fathers were subsequently persuaded to participate.
	Activities: Mothers took turns working with the

group of children. They
eventually hired a teacher
and found a place for the
group to meet.

CONSEQUENCES:

*Those women were very
important to me in a
social way, a community
way, making me feel who
I was. That's one of the
things about the women's
movement, that there's all
sorts of needs for social
group, community feeling
that it provided for me.
And it gave me a link into
America, too, which was
meaningful as a
foreigner. . . . I would say
that not one of all the
women, with one
exception out of maybe
twenty-five women
involved in those play
groups* [the group for her
older child and the second
group for her younger]
*when they started, were in
the women's movement.
There was one other
woman I know* [in
addition to Sarah, herself]
*who came into those play
groups with a clear sense
of saying, "I'm in women's
liberation." At this point*
[in May 1973], *I would*

Personal	Political

Political

say twenty out of twenty-five have some sort of peripheral or central involvement [with the movement]. *. . . And you know, women started demanding that their husbands do a share of the play group and all that sort of thing!*

Sarah credits the play groups with giving her free time to develop her own interests in women's health. When she went back to school full-time in 1972, the other women kept her child in the group without requiring time from her:

And that was something that depended on having those years of putting work into something so that then people were prepared to help me.

Personal

Sarah's husband, who was working for a radical newspaper, was challenged by his female co-workers about his attitudes:

. . . both the way he treated women in his work situations and also the way he dealt with his own children. So . . . they said that if he didn't take care of his own children part

Personal	Political
of the time, he was going to have to take care of the other newspaper children. So, he didn't want to take care of the other newspaper children. . . .	
Sarah's husband chose to care for his own children and started to assume more family responsibilities.	
Summer 1970—Visited her family in Sweden.	
Fall 1970	Took part in attempt to expand the functions of the Women's Abortion Project so that it would confront a wider range of health issues. The name of the project was changed at this time to the Women's Health and Abortion Project. DURATION: The Women's Health and Abortion Project (originally the Women's Abortion Project) was meeting sporadically in May 1973 and producing some literature on abortion. Sarah gradually became less active and left the project in May

Personal	Political

Political

1971, when she felt it had become primarily an abortion-referral business.

TIME COMMITMENT: One to two days a week.

PERSONNEL: Participants in the Women's Abortion Project and other women interested in forming a multigroup health organization.

ACTIVITIES: Several groups were formed, with the Abortion Project conceived as one of the participating groups. One new group planned to produce videotapes on health issues; another bought an old bus to equip as a mobile health unit; and the Women's Health Collective (which Sarah had joined at its inception in 1969) organized women's health courses and produced health leaflets. The Health Organizing Collective was formed at this time.

CONSEQUENCES: With the exception of the Abortion Project, which continued operating under its new name, the Women's Health and Abortion Project, most groups met sporadically and

Personal	Political
	gradually dissolved. One group, the new Health Organizing Collective, continued as a separate entity.
December 1970	Joined the Health Organizing Collective, which had been formed in November, to "try and work around institutions," as part of the revised Women's Health and Abortion Project.

DURATION: Functioning in May 1973.

PERSONNEL:

> *The impetus was from women who came out of the welfare rights movement. . . . They were white middle-class women, some of whom were sort of social workers, mental health workers, who had felt the limits of working with a predominantly black organization and doing fund-raising and that sort of thing, who had been engaged in what they thought of as somebody else's struggle, and had experienced the women's movement in some way so that they wanted to work around their own struggles.*

Personal	*Political*
	TIME COMMITMENT: Two evenings a week and approximately one day (less in 1973).
	ACTIVITIES: One evening a week was spent on consciousness raising; a second evening was devoted to work. The group produced pamphlets, conducted a health survey, gave speeches on women's health issues, produced radio programs and a television program, and helped the Abortion Project with abortion referrals.
	CONSEQUENCES: When the Collective began in 1970, approximately half the participants were working in health-related areas. The other women moved into professional health work during their time with the group:

> *In the women's health movement as a whole, people who got into activism about abortion or something like this moved into some sort of medical field: social workers who started working with health institutions or people who went to nursing school, or*

Personal	Political
	me going to public health school. One of the women in the original group [the Women's Health Collective] *has just been accepted at medical school and one woman at the Health Organizing Collective has just been accepted at the Stony Brook physician's assistant program.*
1971	Continued participation in consciousness-raising group; Women's Health and Abortion Project [until May]; Health Organizing Collective; and second cooperative play group.
Winter 1971	Taught several women's health courses at the Women's Medical Center.
Summer Husband took their son hitchhiking across the country with him, while Sarah and her daughter lived with a family in Chicago.	Worked at the Women's Union in Chicago: planned two women's health courses for their Liberation School; exchanged information with abortion people there; discussed coordination of women's health programs.
Fall 1971	Sarah and her husband began to discuss forming a commune with another family. Discussions gradually included a third family:

... there were dissatisfactions in living as we did. Increasingly, it seemed to me that my independence depended on my husband's dependence ... that he was very responsible toward the children, took care of them a lot, but the more he did that, the more I was dependent on him, and the more we functioned as a nuclear family. ... The more he got into the kids, it became this thing, *and I would be waiting for him to get back in order to get to my meeting. It seemed rational in terms of child care to be living with a group, and then the woman wouldn't be so dependent on the other person. ... But it was also true that communes to me in the early days, with the rhetoric that went with them and lots of the sorts of people who tried them first, who were much more far out, were very threatening to me. And it wasn't until I could really see a way in which I could continue*

> *who I was, and the
> security that one could do
> it that way, that I could
> see I could get out of it
> the things that I wanted,
> that I could see a chance
> of doing it. . . . I didn't
> want to totally change my
> life style. I didn't want
> other people to be parents
> to my children. I didn't
> want* not *to be a couple
> completely in any way.
> And I wanted a lot of
> privacy. . . . I felt that we
> could build a commune
> on our mutual needs for
> child care and friendship.*

January 1972   Applied to Columbia
University's School of Public
Health to enter their MPH
(master's degree in public
health) program.

> *I knew I wanted to start
> working again, and I
> wasn't quite sure how, and
> I didn't want to go back
> to a lab. . . . I felt I knew
> a certain amount from
> the patient stuff we'd
> been doing* [in the health
> groups], *that I knew a
> certain amount about a
> variety of health
> institutions, the way they
> worked. But there was a
> lot more I didn't*

	know. . . . And I wanted a way in which I would have a sort of structured way of reading a lot. And I wanted to learn what they were teaching about. And the other thing was I had worked a lot with Health Pac [a radical health organization] . . . *but somewhat mistrusted the constant radical view* [of the American health system]. *It wasn't that I thought they were wrong but I had no perspective in which to put it.*
February 1972	Taught course on women in a New Jersey college during spring semester. Taught course on women's health at Women's Medical Center.
June	Helped organize Health Conference held in Philadelphia. DURATION: Planning started in April; conference held in June. PERSONNEL: Run by Philadelphia Women's Health Collective. Feminist health groups, rather than individuals, from Maine to Washington, D.C., were invited: consumer groups; consciousness-raising groups on health; writing groups;

Personal	*Political*
	groups that gave health courses.
	ACTIVITIES: Group tactics, plans, and ideas were shared during a series of workshops.
	CONSEQUENCES: Participants enjoyed the conference, but Sarah was disappointed that a communication network was not formed. The majority of participants were overextended and had no time to volunteer for additional work.
September 1972	Started at Columbia University's School of Public Health as a full-time student for an MPH.
December	Moved into commune with two other families.
	DURATION: Discussions began in the fall of 1971. A large brownstone on the upper West Side of Manhattan was bought and the families moved into the house a year later.
	PERSONNEL: Three families: six adults, five children. The women all have or are working on graduate degrees; the men work, as a writer, college instructor, and clinical psychologist.
	ACTIVITIES: Every individual,

adult and child, has his or
her own room. Adults share
on a rotating basis child
care, house cleaning, food
shopping, cooking, house
renovation (cabinet making,
painting, sanding, etc.).
CONSEQUENCES:

*There are problems, but
there would be problems
anyway. And I certainly
feel I can't imagine going
back. We may live here
the rest of our lives
because going back to live
by ourselves, or whatever,
would be quite impossible.*

1973   Participated in the Health
                              Organizing Collective.
                              Several women were working
                              or attending school full-
                              time, so activities were
                              somewhat curtailed.

May   Graduated from Columbia
                              with an MPH (master's
                              degree in Public Health).
                              Started to look for a job, on
                              a part-time basis, so she
                              could spend time with the
                              children. Preferred working
                              for a health agency or
                              institution, but was also
                              interviewing for teaching
                              positions.

Notes

INTRODUCTION

1. Abner Cohen, *Two Dimensional Man: An Essay on the Anthropology of Power and Symbolism in Complex Society* (Berkeley and Los Angeles: University of California Press, 1974), p. 68.

2. Erving Goffman, "The Moral Career of the Mental Patient," in *Asylums: Essays on the Social Situation of Mental Patients and Other Inmates* (Garden City, N.Y.: Doubleday Anchor, 1961).

3. Cohen, *Two Dimensional Man*, p. 65.

4. I am indebted to Ruth Cowan for this insight.

5. Celestine Ware, *Woman Power: The Movement for Women's Liberation* (New York: Tower, 1970); Jo Freeman, *The Politics of Women's Liberation* (New York: David McKay, 1975); Judith Hole and Ellen Levine, *Rebirth of Feminism* (New York: Quadrangle, 1971).

6. Maren Lockwood Carden, *The New Feminism* (New York: Russell Sage Foundation, 1974), p. 177.

7. Ibid., p. 176.

8. Ibid., p. 178.

CHAPTER 1

1. Georg Simmel, "The Web of Group-Affiliations," in *Conflict and the Web of Group-Affiliations*, trans. R. Bendix (New York: Free Press, 1962), pp. 180–84.

2. Peter L. Berger and Thomas Luckmann, *The Social Construction of Reality: A Treatise in the Sociology of Knowledge* (Garden City, N.Y.: Doubleday Anchor, 1967), p. 157.

3. Ibid., p. 157.

4. Luther P. Gerlach and Virginia H. Hine, *People, Power, Change: Movements of Social Transformation* (Indianapolis and New York: Bobbs-Merrill, 1970), pp. 110–37.

5. Berger and Luckmann, *Social Construction of Reality*, p. 157.

6. Ibid., pp. 158–59.

CHAPTER 2

1. Carolyn Stoloff, "Who Joins Women's Liberation?" *Psychiatry* 36 (1973): 334.

2. Robin Morgan, "Goodby to All That," in *Masculine/ Feminine: Readings in Sexual Mythology and the Liberation of Women*, ed. Betty Roszak and Theodore Roszak (New York: Harper Colophon, 1969), p. 245.

3. Esther Newton and Shirley Walton, "The Personal Is Political: Consciousness-Raising and Personal Change in the Women's Liberation Movement" (Paper delivered at the meeting of the American Anthropological Association, New York City, 1971), pp. 23, 24.

4. Stoloff, "Who Joins Women's Liberation?"

5. Luther P. Gerlach and Virginia H. Hine, *People, Power, Change: Movements of Social Transformation* (Indianapolis and New York: Bobbs-Merrill, 1970), p. xxi.

6. Peter L. Berger and Thomas Luckmann, *The Social Construction of Reality: A Treatise in the Sociology of Knowledge* (Garden City, N.Y.: Doubleday Anchor, 1967), pp. 150–53.

7. Kate Millett, *Sexual Politics* (Garden City, N.Y.: Doubleday, 1970).

8. Clifford Geertz, "Ideology as a Cultural System," in *The Interpretation of Cultures* (New York: Basic, 1973), p. 232.

9. Betty Friedan, *The Feminine Mystique* (New York: W. W. Norton, 1963).

10. Berger and Luckmann, *Social Construction of Reality*, p. 153.

11. The concept of "comparison group" comes from the discussion of reference groups in Robert K. Merton, *Social Theory and Social Structure* (New York: Free Press, 1968), p. 337.

CHAPTER 3

1. Esther Newton and Shirley Walton, "The Personal Is Political: Consciousness-Raising and Personal Change in the Women's Liberation Movement" (Paper delivered at the meeting of the American Anthropological Association, New York City, 1971), p. 25.

2. Ibid., p. 28.

3. Ibid., p. 30.

4. See Pamela Allen, *Free Space: A Perspective on the Small Group in Women's Liberation* (New York: Times Change Press, 1970), for a discussion of the formation and functions of a consciousness-raising group.

5. Newton and Walton, "Personal Is Political," appendix B.

6. A classic exposition of the feminist view of housework is found in Pat Mainardi, "The Politics of Housework," in *Notes from the Second Year: Women's Liberation* (New York: Radical Feminists, 1970).

7. See Vivian Gornick, "The Next Great Moment in History Is Theirs," in *The Bold New Women*, ed. Barbara Wasserman (New York: Fawcett, 1970), for a feminist explanation of a similar inability to act.

8. Newton and Walton make a similar point in "Personal Is Political," p. 49.

CHAPTER 4

1. Letty Cottin Pogrebin, "Competing with Women," *MS* 1, no. 1 (1972): 78.

2. Lionel Tiger, *Men in Groups* (New York: Vintage, 1970); Sigmund Freud, "Femininity," in *New Introductory Lectures on Psychoanalysis*, trans. and ed. James Strachey (New York: W. W. Norton, 1965), p. 134. For the feminist view, see Judith M. Bardwick and Elizabeth Douvan, "Ambivalence: The Socialization of Women," in *Women in Sexist Society*, ed. Vivian Gornick and Barbara K. Moran (New York: Basic, 1971), pp. 147, 159.

3. Georg Simmel, "The Web of Group-Affiliations," in *Conflict and the Web of Group-Affiliations*, trans. R. Bendix (New York: Free Press, 1964), p. 180.

4. Esther Newton and Shirley Walton, "The Personal Is Political: Consciousness-Raising and Personal Change in the Women's Liberation Movement" (Paper delivered at the meeting of the American Anthropological Association, New York City, 1971), p. 4.

5. Sidney Abbott and Barbara Love, *Sappho Was a Right-On Woman: A Liberated View of Lesbianism* (New York: Stein & Day, 1972), p. 150.

6. Pamela Allen, *Free Space: A Perspective on the Small Group in Women's Liberation* (New York: Times Change Press, 1970), p. 26.

7. Ingrid Bengis, "Love," *MS* 1, no. 5 (1972): 70.

8. Both quotations come from Newton and Walton, "Personal Is Political," p. 40.

9. Peter L. Berger and Hansfried Kellner, "Marriage and the Construction of Reality," *Diogenes* 46 (1964): 1.

10. Ibid., p. 4.

11. Women's Collective, "Consciousness-Raising" (n.d.).

12. Newton and Walton, "Personal Is Political," p. 40.

13. Karen Durbin, "Casualties of the Sex War," *Village Voice*, 6 April 1972, p. 15.

14. Bengis, "Love," p. 125.

15. David Gutmann, "The Premature Gerontocracy: Scenes of Aging and Death in the Youth Culture," *Social Research* 39, no. 3 (1972): 441.

16. Bengis, "Love," p. 125.

17. Linda Wolfe, "When Men Lose Interest in Sex," *McCall's*, April 1973, p. 30.

18. Gutmann, "Premature Gerontocracy," p. 441.

19. M. Garland Harris, "Ethnography of a Consciousness-Raising Group" (New York: Columbia School of General Studies, n.d.).

20. Abbott and Love, "Sappho," p. 155.

21. Shulamith Firestone, *The Dialectic of Sex: The Case for Feminist Revolution* (New York: William Morrow, 1970), p. 272.

22. Ibid., p. 155.

23. Ann Koedt, "The Myth of the Vaginal Orgasm," in *Notes*

from the Second Year: Women's Liberation (New York: Radical Feminists, 1970), p. 41.

24. Ingrid Bengis, *Combat in the Erogenous Zone* (New York: Alfred A. Knopf, 1972).

25. Shulamith Firestone, "Love," in *Notes from the Second Year: Women's Liberation* (New York: Radical Feminists, 1970), p. 27.

CHAPTER 5

1. Judith Hole and Ellen Levine, *Rebirth of Feminism* (New York, Quadrangle, 1971), p. 240.

2. Sidney Abbott and Barbara Love, *Sappho Was a Right-On Woman: A Liberated View of Lesbianism* (New York: Stein & Day, 1972), p. 157.

3. Quoted in ibid., p. 152.

4. Brenda Hureau, "Male Friends," *New York Radical Feminists Newsletter* 3, no. 11 (1973): 2.

5. Sigmund Freud, "Femininity," in *New Introductory Lectures on Psychoanalysis*, trans. and ed. James Strachey (New York: W. W. Norton, 1965); Helene Deutsch, *The Psychology of Women: A Psychoanalytic Interpretation*, 2 vols. (New York: Grune & Stratton, 1944).

6. Horney broke with her mentor, Freud, on his interpretation of the psychology of women. See Karen Horney, "Feminine Psychology," in *New Ways in Psychoanalysis* (New York: W. W. Norton, 1939); and Clara M. Thompson, *On Women* (New York and Scarborough, Ontario: New American Library, 1971).

7. Freud, "Femininity"; Deutsch, *Psychology of Women*; Thompson, *On Women*.

8. Alexandra Symonds, "The Women's Liberation Movement" (Paper presented at Stritch School of Medicine, Loyola University, 1971).

9. See Naomi Weisstein, "Psychology Constructs the Female," in *Women in Sexist Society*, ed. Vivian Gornick and Barbara K. Moran (New York: Basic, 1971); Judith M. Bardwick and Elizabeth Douvan, "Ambivalence: The Socialization of Women," in ibid.; Broverman et al., "Sex-Role Stereotypes and Clinical Judgements of Mental Health," *Journal of Consulting and Clinical Psychology* 34, no. 1 (1970): 1–7.

10. Peter L. Berger and Thomas Luckmann, *The Social*

Construction of Reality: A Treatise in the Sociology of Knowledge (Garden City, N.Y.: Doubleday Anchor, 1967), pp. 158–59.

11. Ingrid Bengis, *Combat in the Erogenous Zone* (New York: Alfred A. Knopf, 1972), p. 188.

12. Abbott and Love, *Sappho*, pp. 153–54.

13. Luther P. Gerlach and Virginia H. Hine, *People, Power, Change: Movements of Social Transformation* (Indianapolis and New York: Bobbs-Merrill, 1970), pp. 99–158.

14. Ibid., p. 135.

15. See Abbott and Love, *Sappho*, p. 137.

16. Martha Shelley, "Notes of a Radical Lesbian," in *Sisterhood Is Powerful: An Anthology of Writings from the Women's Liberation Movement*, ed. Robin Morgan (New York: Vintage, 1970), p. 307.

17. See Anne Koedt, "Lesbianism and Feminism," in *Notes from the Third Year: Women's Liberation* (New York: Notes from the Second Year, 1971), p. 88; Hole and Levine, *Rebirth of Feminism*, pp. 240–41.

18. To do this, we must follow Abbott and Love's division of lesbians into "political" and "premovement" and acknowledge that at this stage we do not know what, if any, differences exist between the two groups. *Sappho*, p. 153.

19. Ibid., pp. 147–49.

20. Berger and Luckmann, *Social Construction of Reality*, pp. 158–59.

CHAPTER 6

1. Erving Goffman, "The Nature of Deference and Demeanor," in *Interaction Ritual* (Garden City, N.Y.: Doubleday Anchor, 1967), p. 77.

2. Erving Goffman, *Behavior in Public Places: Notes on the Social Organization of Gatherings* (New York: Free Press, 1966), p. 222.

3. John Lyons, *Introduction to Theoretical Linguistics* (Cambridge, England: Cambridge University Press, 1968), p. 79.

4. Goffman, "Behavior," p. 12.

5. See Michael Argyle, "Non-Verbal Communication in Human Social Interaction," in *Non-Verbal Communication*, ed. Robert A. Hinde (Cambridge, England: Cambridge University Press, 1973); Gregory Bateson, *Steps Towards an Ecology of Mind*

(New York: Ballantine, 1972), p. 413; Goffman, *Behavior,* p. 12.

6. For example, see Edmund Bergler, *Fashion and the Unconscious* (New York: Robert Brunner, 1953); J. C. Flugel, *The Psychology of Clothes* (London: Hogarth Press, 1930).

7. S. F. Nadel, *The Theory of Social Structure* (London: Cohen & West, 1957), p. 20.

8. See Judith Hole and Ellen Levine, *Rebirth of Feminism* (New York: Quadrangle, 1971), pp. 229–30.

9. Nadel, *Social Structure,* p. 69.

10. Georg Simmel, "The Web of Group-Affiliations," in *Conflict and the Web of Group-Affiliations,* trans. R. Bendix (New York: Free Press, 1964), p. 150.

11. See Vivian Gornick and Barbara K. Moran, *Women in Sexist Society* (New York: Basic, 1971), p. 3, pp. 118–30.

12. Nadel, *Social Structure,* p. 69.

13. Goffman, "Deference and Demeanor," p. 56.

14. Dana Densmore, "Chivalry—the Iron Hand in the Velvet Glove," (Pittsburgh, Pa.: KNOW reprint, 1969), pp. 1–2.

15. Margaret Mead, *Male and Female: A Study of the Sexes in a Changing World* (New York: Dell, 1968), pp. 86–97; Bateson, *Ecology of Mind,* p. 109.

16. See Sidney Abbott and Barbara Love, *Sappho Was a Right-On Woman: A Liberated View of Lesbianism* (New York: Stein & Day, 1972), pp. 94–98.

17. Nadel, *Social Structure,* p. 49.

18. Fredrik Barth, "Introduction," in *Ethnic Groups and Boundaries: The Social Organization of Culture Difference,* trans. Fredrik Barth (London: George Allen & Unwin, 1969), p. 14.

CHAPTER 7

1. Mary Miles Frossard Gallagher, "Women's Liberation: Social Movement in a Complex Society" (Ph.D. dissertation, University of Colorado, 1973), p. 8.

2. Jo Freeman, "The New Feminism," *The Nation,* March 9, 1974: 298. For an informed and insightful discussion of the origins of the contemporary American Women's Movement see Jo Freeman, *The Politics of Women's Liberation* (New York: David McKay, 1975), pp. 44–102. Freeman disagrees with the division of the movement into a pragmatic women's rights branch and a utopian women's liberation branch. She believes that the difference between the branches is one of age, style and structure

and contends that the ideology of the older branch of the movement is as revolutionary as that of the younger. The primary political difference between the two branches, states Freeman, is that the younger branch devotes itself primarily to group maintenance activities, where the existence of the small group is valued more highly than its social change functions, while the older branch devotes itself to goal achievement, seeking and achieving tangible changes in the social structure.

3. Judith Hole and Ellen Levine, *Rebirth of Feminism* (New York: Quadrangle, 1971), p. 2; Maren Lockwood Carden, *The New Feminist Movement* (New York: Russell Sage Foundation, 1974), p. 2.

4. Maren Lockwood Carden, "Feminism in 1975: The Non-Establishment, the Establishment, and the Future" (Report prepared for the Co-ordinating Committee on Women's Programs, Ford Foundation, March 1976), pp. 2–3.

5. Ibid., p. 64.

6. Gallagher, "Women's Liberation"; Carden, *New Feminist Movement*.

7. See Cohen for a description of the difference between formally and informally organized groups. Abner Cohen, *Two Dimensional Man* (Berkeley and Los Angeles: University of California Press, 1974), pp. 66–68.

CHAPTER 8

1. See Ralph Linton, "Nativistic Movements," *American Anthropologist* 45 (1943): 230–40; Fred W. Voget, "Toward a Classification of Cult Movements: Some Further Contributions," *Man* 59 (1959): 26–28; Anthony F. C. Wallace, "Revitalization Movements," *American Anthropologist* 58 (1956): 264–81; Sylvia L. Thrupp, ed., *Millennial Dreams in Action: Studies in Revolutionary Religious Movements* (New York: Schocken, 1970); Peter Worsley, *The Trumpet Shall Sound: A Study of "Cargo" Cults in Melanesia*, rev. ed. (New York: Schocken, 1968); I. C. Jarvie, "Theories of Cargo Cults: A Critical Analysis," *Oceania* 34, nos. 1 and 2 (1963): 1–31, 108–36; Weston La Barre, "Materials for a History of Studies of Crisis Cults: A Bibliographic Essay," *Current Anthropology* 12, no. 1 (1971): 43–44.

2. Anthony F. C. Wallace, *Religion: An Anthropological View* (New York: Random House, 1966), p. 164.

3. David F. Aberle, *The Peyote Religion among the Navaho* (Chicago: Aldine, 1966), pp. 315–22.

4. Neil J. Smelser, *Theory of Collective Behavior* (New York: Free Press, 1962).

5. Ibid., p. 120.

6. Luther P. Gerlach and Virginia H. Hine, *People, Power, Change: Movements of Social Transformation* (Indianapolis and New York: Bobbs-Merrill, 1970).

7. The classic formulation of this is found in Max Weber, *The Theory of Social and Economic Organization*, ed. and trans. Talcott Parsons (New York: Free Press, 1964). Also see Wallace, "Revitalization Movements"; Worsley, *Trumpet Shall Sound*; and Peter Lawrence, *Road Belong Cargo: A Study of the Cargo Movement in the Southern Madang District, New Guinea* (New York: Humanities Press, 1964).

8. Gerlach and Hine, *People, Power, Change*, p. 35.

9. These figures came from the *New York Times*, 24 January 1976, p. 20. In 1975, a bitter dispute that had been simmering below the surface in NOW erupted. Thirteen leaders, dissatisfied with NOW's movement toward a more radical posture, split from the group and formed a new organization called Womansurge. Many of the ideas and practices objected to by the secessionists resembled utopian women's liberation attempts to down-play leadership, eliminate hierarchy, and forge a revolution.

10. Gerlach and Hine, *People, Power, Change*, pp. 38–41.

11. Ibid., p. 41.

12. A discussion of this type of network and how it might be graphed can be found in J. A. Barnes, "Class and Committee in a Norwegian Parish," *Human Relations* 7 (1954): 39–58.

13. The concept of "sociometric star" is found in J. L. Moreno, *Who Shall Survive? Foundations of Sociometry, Group Psychotherapy and Sociodrama* (Beacon, N.Y.: Beacon House, 1953). Moreno also graphed networks, in a somewhat different fashion from Barnes.

14. See Sidney Abbott and Barbara Love, *Sappho Was a Right-On Woman: A Liberated View of Lesbianism* (New York: Stein & Day, 1972), chap. 5, for discussion of NOW factionalism on the issue of lesbianism.

15. Gerlach and Hine, *People, Power, Change*, p. 72.

16. For example, see Worsley, *Trumpet Shall Sound*; Lawrence, *Road Belong Cargo*; Theodore Schwartz, "The Paliau Movement in the Admiralty Islands," American Museum of Natural History Anthropological Papers 49, pt. 2 (New York,

1962). Similar points have been made by Mary Miles Frossard Gallagher, "Women's Liberation: Social Movement in a Complex Society" (Ph.D. dissertation, University of Colorado, 1973), p. 66; and Gerlach and Hine, *People, Power, Change*, p. 38.

17. Abner Cohen, *Two-Dimensional Man: An Essay on the Anthropology of Power and Symbolism in Complex Society* (Berkeley and Los Angeles: University of California Press, 1974), p. 68.

CHAPTER 9

1. Dorothy Tennov, "Feminism, Psychotherapy and Professionalism" (Paper delivered at the Feminist Psychology Conference, City University Graduate Center, New York City, n.d.).

2. Anselma dell'Olio, "Divisiveness and Self-Destruction in the Women's Movement" (Speech given at the Congress to Unite Women, New York City, 1970).

3. The following discussion owes much to an article by Jo Freeman, "The Tyranny of Structurelessness," *Second Wave* 2, no. 1 (1972): 20–42, reprinted in *MS* 2 (July 1973): 76–89.

4. Personal letter from a former member of the university action group.

5. Bailey describes similar values in peasant ideologies: "No matter what goes on in reality, the public life of a peasant community is ideally conducted in the idiom of cooperation: fellow villagers in India are known as 'village-brothers,' public administration is conducted through consensual procedures which emphasize solidarity rather than through the divisive procedure of majority voting." F. G. Bailey, *Stratagems and Spoils: A Social Anthropology of Politics* (New York: Schocken, 1969), pp. 148–49.

6. Luther P. Gerlach and Virginia H. Hine, *People, Power, Change: Movements of Social Transformation* (Indianapolis and New York: Bobbs-Merrill, 1970), pp. 183–97.

7. Freeman, "Tyranny," p. 22.

CHAPTER 10

1. Jo Freeman, "The Tyranny of Structurelessness," *Second Wave* 2, no. 1 (1972): 20–42, reprinted in *MS* 2 (July 1973): 76–89; Maren Lockwood Carden, *The New Feminist Movement* (New York: Russell Sage Foundation, 1974), chap. 7.

2. Freeman, "Tyranny," p. 20.

3. Carden, *New Feminist Movement*, p. 86. Freeman suggests that women's liberation structures and strategies were inherited from the student, peace, and civil rights movements. Jo Freeman, "The Origins of the Women's Liberation Movement," *American Journal of Sociology* 78, no. 4 (1973): 1–20.

4. F. G. Bailey, *Stratagems and Spoils: A Social Anthropology of Politics* (New York: Schocken, 1969), p. 147.

5. Victor W. Turner, *The Ritual Process: Structure and Anti-Structure* (Chicago: Aldine, 1969), p. 96.

6. Ibid., p. 131.

7. Barbara G. Myerhoff, "Organization and Ecstasy: Deliberate and Accidental Communitas among Huichol Indians and American Youth," in *Symbol and Politics in Communal Ideology*, ed. Sally Falk Morre and Barbara G. Myerhoff (Ithaca: Cornell University Press, 1975), p. 33.

8. Ibid., p. 33. I have replaced "man" with "woman" and "his" with "her" when appropriate.

9. See E. R. Leach, "Symbolic Representation of Time," in *Rethinking Anthropology* (London: Athelone, 1966); and Myerhoff, "Organization and Ecstasy."

10. Martin Buber, quoted by Turner, *Ritual Process*, p. 127.

11. Esther Newton and Shirley Walton, "The Personal Is Political: Consciousness-Raising and Personal Change in the Women's Liberation Movement" (Paper delivered at the meeting of the American Anthropoligocal Association, New York City, 1971), pp. 29–31.

12. Terri Shultz, "Last Word," *Viva*, May 1974, p. 120. This is an article about the feelings of women who become feminists. My point is that, although the concept of communitas is not recognized as such in the women's movement, the feeling of communion and support is recognized, discussed, and valued.

13. Turner, *Ritual Process*, pp. 106–7.

14. Barbara G. Myerhoff, "Organization and Ecstasy: The Dialectic of Communitas and Structure" (Paper delivered at the meeting of the American Anthropological Association, New York City, 1971), p. 5b.

15. Sherry Roxanne Turkle, "Symbol and Festival in the 'Evenements de Mai-Juin 1968' " (Paper delivered at the meeting of the American Anthropological Association, New York City, 1971).

16. David Buchdahl, "Inversions of the Middle: Difficulties

and Directions in Symbolizing the Margin" (Paper delivered at the meeting of the American Anthropological Association, New York City, 1971).

17. Luther P. Gerlach and Virginia H. Hine, *People, Power, Change: Movements of Social Transformation* (Indianapolis and New York: Bobbs-Merrill, 1970).

18. Simone de Beauvoir, *The Second Sex*, trans. and ed. H. M. Parshely (London: Jonathan Cape, 1953), pp. 15–16.

19. Helen Mayer Hacker, "Women as a Minority Group," in *Masculine/Feminine: Readings in Sexual Mythology and the Liberation of Women*, ed. Betty Roszak and Theodore Roszak (New York: Harper Colophon, 1969).

20. Victor W. Turner, "Betwixt and Between: The Liminal Period in *Rites de Passage*," in *The Forest of Symbols: Aspects of Ndembu Ritual* (Ithaca: Cornell University Press, 1970), pp. 94–97.

21. Susannah Hoffman, "Social Structure, Women and the Occult" (Paper delivered at the American Anthropological Association, New York City, 1971).

22. Abner Cohen, *Two-Dimensional Man: An Essay on the Anthropology of Power and Symbolism in Complex Society* (Berkeley and Los Angeles: University of California Press, 1974), p. 117.

23. David Bakan, *The Duality of Human Existence: Isolation and Communion in Western Man* (Chicago: Rand McNally, 1966), p. 15.

24. See Ronald W. Hogeland, " 'The Female Appendage': Feminine Life-Styles in America, 1820–1860," *Civil War History* 17, no. 2 (1971); and Gerda Lerner, "The Lady and the Mill Girl: Changes in the Status of Women in the Age of Jackson," *American Studies* 10, no. 1 (1973).

25. Aileen S. Kraditor, *The Ideas of the Woman Suffrage Movement 1890–1920* (Garden City, N. Y: Doubleday Anchor, 1971), p. 91.

26. Lionel Tiger bases an entire book of prehistoric speculation on this attribution. See his *Men in Groups* (New York: Vintage, 1970).

27. Kraditor, *Ideas of Woman Suffrage Movement*, p. 91.

28. Turner, *Ritual Process*, p. 132. Italics added.

29. Ibid., pp. 132–33.

30. Gerlach and Hine observe that although key phrases in the

ideology of a social movement may sound vague to outsiders, to a committed participant the phrases have experiential connotations that "are very clear in meaning, can be translated in specific goals, and entail certain behavioral consequences. *People, Power, Change,* p. 170. The experience referred to when the term "elitism" is used is its opposite, communitas.

31. Jo Freeman, "The Tyranny of Structurelessness," *Ms,* July 1973, p. 21.

32. Myerhoff, "Organization and Ecstasy," p. 51.

33. The FEMINISTS, "Organizational Principles and Structure," 1970, p. 1.

34. Melford E. Spiro, *Children of the Kibbutz: A Study in Child Training and Personality* (New York: Schocken, 1966), p. 115.

35. Stanley Diamond, "Kibbutz and Shtetl: The History of an Idea," *Social Problems* 5, no. 2 (1957): 82.

36. Ibid., pp. 85–86.

37. Ibid., p. 74.

38. Anthony F. C. Wallace, "Revitalization Movements," *American Anthropologist* 58 (1956): 264–81.

39. Anthony F. C. Wallace, *Religion: An Anthropological View* (New York: Random House, 1966), p. 161.

40. See Peter Worsley, *The Trumpet Shall Sound: A Study of "Cargo" Cults in Melanesia,* rev. ed. (New York: Schocken, 1968), pp. 170–94, where the author sounds almost embarrassed about finding "millenarian elements" together with "orthodox political" activity. *It is precisely the relationship between the two that is interesting.*

41. The distinction between magical and rational means is found in Ralph Linton, "Nativistic Movements," *American Anthropologist* 45 (1943): 230–40; between nonrealistic and realistic conflict in Lewis A. Coser, *The Functions of Social Conflict* (New York: Free Press, 1956); between status and class issues in Joseph R. Gusfield, *Symbolic Crusade: Status Politics and the American Temperance Movement* (Urbana: University of Illinois Press, 1960); between partial and total change and personal and social change in David F. Aberle, *The Peyote Religion among the Navaho* (Chicago: Aldine, 1966); and between need and value-oriented movements in Neil J. Smelser, *Theory of Collective Behavior* (New York: Free Press, 1962).

42. For example, see Jeanne Humphrey Block, "Conceptions

of Sex Role," in *Selected Studies in Marriage and the Family,* ed. Robert F. Winch and Graham B. Spanier, 4th ed. (New York: Holt, Rinehart and Winston, 1974).

43. For example, see Philadelphia Women's Anthropology Collective, "Some Thoughts on Structure and Organization," *Newsletter of the Women's Caucus of the American Anthropological Association* 1, no. 2 (1972): 1–2; Germaine Greer, *The Female Eunuch* (New York: McGraw-Hill, 1971), p. 300.

44. Carden, *New Feminist Movement,* p. 118, 128.

45. NOW filed the Little League lawsuit in 1973; NOW prepared the ERA kit in 1974; sex discrimination charges were filed at *Newsweek* and *Time* in 1970.

46. The New York Radical Feminists held the Rape speakout in 1971, the Motherhood speakout in 1974; RAT was taken over by a feminist coup in 1970; the sit-in was held at the *Ladies Home Journal* in 1970.

47. Carden, *New Feminist Movement,* p. 170; Judy Sullivan, "Negotiating a Feminist Community," *New York Radical Feminists Newsletter* 3, no. 7 (1973): 3.

CHAPTER 11

1. Elizabeth Janeway, "The Real Second Sex," *Cosmopolitan,* June 1973, pp. 148–64.

2. During the following year, Sarah became involved with a feminist educational health project, and her formal group activity increased.

3. A description of a separatist lesbian feminist community that did provide jobs, substitute families, and a way of life for members is found in Elizabeth Barnhart, "Friends and Lovers in a Countercultural Lesbian Community," in *Old Family/New Family,* ed. Nona Glazer-Malbin (Princeton, N.J.: Van Nostrand, 1975).

4. Judith Hole and Ellen Levine, *Rebirth of Feminism* (New York: Quadrangle, 1971), pp. 145–47.

5. In a report on the state of the women's movement in 1975, Carden states that the women's liberation wing of the movement has disintegrated. Maren Lockwood Carden, *Feminism in 1975: The Non-Establishment, the Establishment, and the Future* (New York: Ford Foundation report prepared for the co-ordinating committee on women's programs, March 1976), p. 3.

6. Catherine Samuels, *Evolution of the Women's Movement*

1971-1974 (New York: Women's Action Alliance, n.d.), p. 8.

7. Personal communication, Ruth Woodcock, assistant executive director, YWCA, City of New York; *Spokeswoman* 2, no. 10 (1972).

8. In 1975, NOW split into a "utopian" faction, seeking revolutionary change, and a "pragmatic" faction, wishing to concentrate on equal treatment for women. Carden, *Feminism in 1975*, p. 64.

9. Samuels, "Evolution," pp. 4–5; Carden, *Feminism in 1975*, p. 2.

10. Ibid., p. 3.

11. *Northwest Passage* (Bellingham, Wash.) 2, no. 4 (29 July– 19 August 1974).

12. *Majority Report* (New York) 4, no. 8 (8 August 1974).

CHAPTER 12

1. William L. O'Neill, "Feminism as a Radical Ideology," in *Dissent: Explorations in the History of American Radicalism*, ed. Alfred E. Young (Dekalb: Northern Illinois University Press, 1968), p. 298.

2. Shulamith Firestone, *The Dialectic of Sex: The Case for Feminist Revolution* (New York: William Morrow, 1970), p. 233; Kate Millett, *Sexual Politics* (Garden City, N.Y: Doubleday, 1970), p. 127; Germaine Greer, *The Female Eunuch* (New York: McGraw-Hill, 1971), p. 232.

3. Janet Malcolm, "Help! Homework for the Liberated Woman," *New Republic*, 10 October 1970.

4. See Bruno Bettleheim, *The Children of the Dream* (New York: Macmillan, 1954); Melford E. Spiro, *Children of the Kibbutz: A Study in Child Training and Personality* (New York: Schocken, 1966); Stanley Diamond, "Kibbutz and Shtetl: The History of an Idea," *Social Problems* 5, no. 2; Yonina Talmon, *Family and Community in the Kibbutz* (Cambridge, Mass.: Harvard University Press, 1972).

5. O'Neill, "Feminism," p. 298.

6. F. G. Bailey, *Stratagems and Spoils: A Social Anthropology of Politics* (New York: Schocken, 1969), p. 131.

7. And organizations such as NON, the National Organization for Non-Parents, receive publicity.

8. Margaret Mead, "Women's Role in Today's World" (New

York: National Council, 1961); "Child Rearing and the Family," *Ekistics* 28, no. 167 (1969): 232–33; "Future Family," *Trans-action* 8 (1971): 50-53.

9. Mead, "Women's Role," p. 8.

10. Ernst Mayr, *Populations, Species and Evolution* (Cambridge, Mass.: Bellknap Press of Harvard University Press, 1970), pp. 406, 410.

11. Helene Deutsch, *The Psychology of Women: A Psychoanalytic Interpretation*, vol. I (New York: Grune & Stratton, 1944).

Index

Monogamy, 183
Moran, Barbara K., 224n
Moreno, J. L., 226n
Morgan, Robin, 23, 219n
Motherhood vs. self-actualization, 52–53, 183–87
Motherhood Speakout, 169
Mothers
  feminist, 22
  relationships with, 42, 43, 44, 47–48, 58–59
Multigroup model. See Structure of the women's movement
Myerhoff, Barbara, 154, 228n, 229n
Myth of the Vaginal Orgasm, The, 70
Nadel, S. F., 224n
National Coalition of Women and Girls in Education, 180
National Council of Jewish Women, 179
National Organization for Non-Parents (NON), 232n
National Organization for Women (NOW), 6, 28, 29, 35, 85, 94–95, 102, 103 f, 109, 113, 116, 117, 119, 168, 179, 180, 185, 226n, 231n, 232n
  committee on the media, 119
National Women's Agenda, 180
Natural look, 89, 155; *see also* Feminist demeanor
Natural selection, negative, 186
Network, feminist, 112–16
New Left, 23–24, 172
Newsweek, 231n
Newton, Esther, 26, 35, 64, 219n, 220n, 221n, 228n
New York Association of Women Business Owners, 180
New York Civil Liberties Union, 180
New York Radical Feminists, 34, 73, 170, 231n
New York Radical Women, 177
New York State abortion law, 174
New York Women's Liberation Center, 5, 34, 37
New York Women's Lobby, 180
No More Fun and Games, 94
Nonverbal communication, 85, 87, 95, 96, 97
Norm-oriented vs. value-oriented beliefs, 106–7, 151, 164–65, 166, 169–70, 182; *see also* Structure of the women's movement
Northwest Passage, 232n

NOW. *See* National Organization for Women
Nuclear family vs. feminism, 69, 156, 183–87; *see also* Marriage
Older vs. younger branch of women's movement. *See* Structure of women's movement
Older Women's Liberation (OWL), 34–35, 64
O'Neill, William N., 183, 185, 232n
Opposition, role of, 141
Oppression of women, 32, 36, 45, 49, 61, 64, 67, 128, 129, 159, 160, 162–63
Passive men, 66–68
Personal is political, 19, 59, 173
Philadelphia Women's Anthropology Collective, 231n
Physicians, attitude toward, 156
Planning meetings, 137–40
Playboy, 184
Pogrebin, Letty Cottin, 220n
Political is personal, 174–77
Political lesbianism, 77
Position of women. *See* Women, position of
Power, attitude toward. *See* Feminist values
President's Commission on the Status of Women, 102
Professional advancement. *See* Motherhood vs. self-actualization
Progressive Household Technicians, 180
Publications, feminist, 116
Psychiatrists, Freudian, 15, 18, 75, 156
Psychology Today, 72
Radical egalitarianism, 129–33, 149, 150, 151, 154, 156, 159, 160–65, 167
Raised consciousness, 15–20, 74; *see also* Consciousness-raising groups
Rape, 181
Rape Speakout, 169
RAT, 231n
Redstockings, 177
Reference group, 32
Reform vs. revolutionary. *See* Structure of the women's movement
Reticulation. *See* Structure of the women's movement
Revitalization movements, 165; *see also* Structure of the women's movement
Revolution, creating a, 146
Ridicule as a social control, 25, 86, 87
Right-to-Life groups, 117

Weber, Max, 226n
Weisstein, Naomi, 222n
Widows, 27
WITCH, 177
Wolfe, Linda, 221n
Womansurge, 226n
Women
  centers for, 115–16
  clothing and, 88–92
  collectives for, 221n
  competition between, 56–57, 88
  as a group, 18, 31–32, 50–51, 170
  marginality of, 157
  as polluting, 157
  position of, 17
  relationships to other women, 48–51,
    56–60
  studies classes, 33, 116
  suffragists, 7, 21, 25
    see also Feminist demeanor, Femi-
    nist symbolism, Feminist values
Women's caucuses, 178

Women's Equity Action League
  (WEAL), 180
Women's liberation action group
  activist core of, 133–36
  case study of, 122–48
  data on participants, 147–48
Women's liberation group-as-a-way-of-
  life, 136–40, 174–87
Women's liberation and women's rights,
  differences between, 102–4, 166–70,
  171, 182, 183, 224n, 231n; see also
  Norm-oriented vs. value-oriented
  beliefs
Women's movement, structure of. See
  Structure of the women's movement
"Women's way." See Feminist values
Women's Wear Daily, 90
Woodcock, Ruth, 232
Worsley, Peter, 225n, 226n, 230n
Young Lords, 179
Young Women's Christian Association
  (YWCA), 179